Twayne's English Authors Series

Sylvia E. Bowman, *Editor*
INDIANA UNIVERSITY

Fanny Burney

Fanny Burney

By MICHAEL E. ADELSTEIN

University of Kentucky

Twayne Publishers, Inc.   ::   New York

To the Memory
of my Father:
SAMUEL ADELSTEIN

Preface

ALTHOUGH nearly all books on eighteenth-century English literature or the history of the English novel mention Fanny Burney, critical discussions of her literary contribution have been sparse and superficial. Several reasons account for this neglect. Fanny's voluminous diaries, invaluable source-books of material about people, places, and manners, stand outside the proper pale of *belles lettres*. Her novels, including the well-known *Evelina*, are obscured by the major works of Daniel Defoe, Samuel Richardson, Henry Fielding, Tobias Smollett, and Laurence Sterne. And her plays, excluding a feeble tragedy, exist only in manuscripts.

This study purports neither to discover Fanny Burney nor to exaggerate her importance, tendencies common in books on minor figures. Instead, it is designed to attract new readers to Fanny Burney's works, to guide them in understanding her strengths and weaknesses as a writer, and to help them in appreciating her literary achievement and in realizing her historical significance. To those already acquainted with Fanny Burney, this study hopes to provide an interesting, inclusive, and incisive analysis and assessment of her works.

In describing, examining, and evaluating Fanny's writings, I have integrated them with biographical material instead of organizing them according to genre or theme. This approach is most helpful because much of what she wrote concerned herself, her family, and her friends. In addition, as this study shows, her work reflects Fanny's own social and economic problems; and its nature and direction were drastically affected by the violent reaction of her father and Mr. Crisp to her first play, *The Witlings*.

I may have taken some liberties in referring to Frances Burney, later Mme d'Arblay, as Fanny. Certainly no disrespect is implied. Few people speak or write about her as Frances, and even fewer identify her by the married name of d'Arblay, although it appears often in indices. To Dr. Johnson and to most writers since, she has been Fanny. So she is called here.

To study Fanny Burney is to become enormously indebted to the meticulous and exhaustive work of Dr. Joyce Hemlow in her indispensable *History of Fanny Burney.* This dedicated scholar has examined about eight thousand unpublished family letters, including some one thousand by Fanny, that are available only in libraries and private collections in this country and abroad. Besides being grateful to Professor Hemlow, I am also indebted to numerous people and institutions. I would like to express my appreciation to Dr. John D. Gordan, curator of the Berg Collection, and to the officials of the New York Public Library for allowing me to read and quote from their valuable Burney manuscripts; to the University of Kentucky for granting me a Summer Research Fellowship; to Dr. Sylvia Bowman for her understanding and her aid in editing; to Professor Alfred Crabb, Jr. for his proofreading assistance; and to my wife, Carol, for succor and support with this study and myself during many trying days.

MICHAEL E. ADELSTEIN

University of Kentucky

Contents

Preface

Chronology

1. The Young Diarist   13
2. A Young Lady's Entrance into the World   28
3. A Young Author's Entrance into the World   45
4. The Death of a Comedy and Birth of a Novel   58
5. A Novel of Love, Pride, and Money   64
6. A Lady Enters Court Life   74
7. A Husband, a Child, and a Novel   90
8. Playing at Playwriting   105
9. A Wandering Author   117
10. Exciting Adventures and Disappointing Memoirs   130
11. A Recapitulation   147

Notes and References   155

Selected Bibliography   163

Index   167

Chronology

1752   Frances Burney was born on June 13 in King's Lynn, England.

1760   Family moved to Poland Street, London.

1762   Death of Fanny's mother.

1767   Burning of Fanny's first novel, *The History of Caroline Evelyn.*

1768   Beginning of diary.

1770   Began practice of writing lengthy journal letters to Mr. Crisp and Susan.

1778   Publication of *Evelina.*

1778–
1783   Visited Streatham upon numerous occasions, staying for weeks and occasionally months with Dr. Johnson and the Thrales.

1779   Completion of *The Witlings,* unpublished comedy.

1782   Publication of *Cecilia.*

1785   Friendship with Mrs. Delany.

1786–
1791   Served as Second Keeper of the Robes to Queen Charlotte, wife of King George III. In 1790, completed *Edwy and Elgiva, Hubert De Vere, The Siege of Pevensey,* and started *Elberta;* her four tragedies.

1793   Married Alexandre d'Arblay in Mickleham on July 28. Wrote *Brief Reflections relative to the Emigrant French Clergy.*

1794   Birth of son, Alexander d'Arblay, December 18.

1796   Publication of *Camilla.*

1798   Completion of *Love and Fashion,* unpublished comedy.

1800   Completion of *A Busy Day,* unpublished comedy.

1801   Completion of *Love and Fashion,* unpublished comedy.

1802   Lived in France, mainly in Paris, during war with England.

1812   Returned to London.

1814 Publication of *The Wanderer*. Death of father. Moved to France.

1815 Flight from Paris to Brussels before advancing Napoleon. Returned to England.

1818 Death of husband.

1832 Publication of *The Memoirs of Dr. Burney*.

1837 Death of son.

1840 Died on January 6 in London.

1843–
1846 Posthumous publication of *Diary and Letters of Madame d'Arblay* (7 vols).

1889 Posthumous publication of *The Early Diary of Frances Burney* (2 vols).

CHAPTER 1

The Young Diarist

AS a fifteen-year-old girl, Fanny Burney picked up her pen to write about her "thoughts, manners, acquaintances and actions." As an eighty-seven-year-old novelist, biographer, diarist, and disappointed playwright, she put it down, completing a life more eventful than those of her own heroines. During this period of seventy-odd years, she "scribbled" away indefatigably to preserve for herself, her family, and a few close friends a picture of the great and the near great. In so doing, she left an account of her own experiences, describing interestingly and vividly what happened to a shy, retiring person who came to be well known as a novelist, closely acquainted with Dr. Johnson, unhappily employed by Queen Charlotte and George III, blissfully married to an emigre French general, and seriously endangered by Napoleon's drive from Elba to Waterloo. She saw the world through perspicacious, satirical, and prudish eyes. She wrote mainly in a natural, refreshing, ebullient manner. What she viewed and heard are reported for others to read and enjoy. What she thought and felt are often omitted for personal reasons.

To peruse her works is to live in an age glorious in elegance, smug in self-assurance, brutal in social indifference, and brilliant in accomplishments. That Fanny Burney preserved the period for posterity in her diaries makes her important to political and social historians. That she was concerned in her novels primarily with the role of women, and with the manners and morals of daily social life, makes her important to literary historians. That she wrote with artistry and sincerity, with vividness and originality, with humor and intelligence, and with vitality and clarity makes her interesting and important as a writer to all readers. Her achievement is limited in scope, marred with blemishes, and inconsistent in quality. Yet her books continue to be printed in hardcover and paperback; to be quoted in biographical, historical,

13

and literary works; and to be read in classrooms and living rooms. Thus Fanny Burney's fame is clearly established. What remains is to define clearly, to analyze thoroughly, and to evaluate generally her contribution to literature.

I *The Family*

When Fanny Burney began writing to "A Certain Miss Nobody" in her diary at fifteen, she thought little of posterity. Her previous literary efforts including her first novel, *The History of Caroline Evelyn,* had been deliberately committed to a bonfire. This time, having no literary aspirations, she hoped only to provide a permanent record of her youth to enjoy in old age. Life was rich, full, and exciting in the Burney household; Fanny wished to preserve it.

She was a member of a large, interesting, and talented family. Years later, William Hazlitt claimed that the Burney name alone was "a passport to the Temple of Fame" because the family produced "wits, scholars, novelists, musicians, artists, in numbers numberless." [1] Fanny's father, Dr. Charles Burney, became famous as a fine musician, author, composer, and teacher. Dr. Johnson, who knew him well, evaluated him best: "I must question if there is in the world such another man, for mind, intelligence and manners, as Dr. Burney." [2] Dr. Burney's pleasing personality, musical knowledge and ability, reputation as an author, and varied interests attracted to his drawing room a multitude of statesmen and politicians, scientists and explorers, musicians and singers, artists and writers, and others of fame and fashion. Their frequent visits to his house were a tribute to a man who rose by his wits and industry from being an apprentice to the composer Arne, to serving as a companion to the fashionable Fulke Greville, and finally to striking out for himself as a musician and teacher of music in London.

Burney started his career to support his beautiful but dowerless wife, Esther Sleepe, and their first child, Esther, born before the marriage was registered. His family and income grew larger: James was born in June, 1750; and Charles a year later. When illness necessitated Burney's leaving London, he fortunately found a position as organist at St. Margaret's Church in King's Lynn, a town about a hundred miles from London. Here Fanny was born on June 13, 1752, and here she lived during her childhood.

Eight years later, with his health restored, and with more children, Dr. Burney returned to London. In the house on fashionable Poland Street, the Burneys entertained their old acquaintances; and the children passed their adolescent years. James, the eldest son, went to sea; the first and even a second Charles had died, but a third, born in December, 1757, survived; Esther, Fanny, Susanna Elizabeth (born January, 1755), and Charlotte Ann (born in London in November, 1761) were the remaining six of the nine children that Esther Sleepe bore. There were no more; she died in September, 1762, when Fanny was ten.

For the next two years after their mother's death the children shuttled between their maternal and paternal grandmothers in London, and their mother's friend, Mrs. Stephen Allen, in King's Lynn. Burney, concerned about the girls' education, took two of them—Esther and Hetty (Susanna Elizabeth)—to Paris to learn French. Fanny was left behind because of weak health and the possibility of her converting to Roman Catholicism, the religion of her beloved maternal grandmother. While her two sisters were away at school and her father traveled back and forth to the Continent, Fanny filled the void in her life with "Daddy" Crisp. This friend of her father, a handsome, intelligent, accomplished gentleman, adored Fanny as she did him. Crisp, frustrated and embittered by the failure of his tragedy, *Virginia,* and by the loss of his fortune and health, had left fashionable London to reside in a dilapidated mansion at Chessington in Surrey, where he read and played cards with other paying guests. He seems to have selected Fanny as his favorite Burney child because she shared his interest in literature; because she amused him with her gay spirits and ability to mimic others; and because she wrote witty, entertaining letters. The love that ripened and grew between the two during this period was to provide Crisp with constant pleasure, and Fanny with a wise and valuable counselor.

Soon the family circumstances changed. Mrs. Allen, whose husband had died, purchased a house near where the Burneys lived in London. Friendships developed between the children of the two families and the widowed parents. The handsome Mrs. Allen soon became the second Mrs. Burney; her three children—Stephen, Maria, and Bessy—raised the total of Burney children to nine. Shortly afterwards, Fanny began her diary to record the happy active days with her brothers and sisters, and with the interesting

people who flocked to converse with Dr. Burney and his bright,
stimulating, and attractive second wife.

II The Early Diary: *Characters; Dialogue*

The Early Diary, published in 1889, forty-nine years after
Fanny's death, consists of her diary, journals, and letters, and also
letters to her by Mr. Crisp and her sisters, all written and received
between her fifteenth and her twenty-fifth year (1768–1778).[3]
What characterizes the *Early Diary* is Fanny's ability to describe
people incisively, to write dialogue effectively, and to present
scenes dramatically. In a sentence or two she catches a person's
characteristic traits. At one of her father's parties, for example,
were Mr. Fitzgerald, "a hard featured, tall, hard voiced and hard
mannered Irishman: fond of music, but fonder of *discussing* than
of listening"; his daughter, a good-natured, lively individual, who
"laughs louder than a man, poked her head vehemently, dresses
shockingly, and has a carriage the most *ungain* that ever was
seen"; the famous sculptor Nollekens, "a jolly, fat lisping, laughing, underbred, good humoured man as lives: his merit seems
pretty much confined to his profession, and his language is as
vulgar as his works are elegant"; and Miss B, "a young lady quite
a la mode" with a low, delicate, and mincing voice, hair "higher
than twelve wigs stuck one on the other," and waist "taper and
pinched, evidently," who casts her eyes languishingly and whose
"conversation is very much *the thing*." [4]

Of all the people represented in the *Early Diary* none is as vividly depicted as Dr. Johnson, who appears at length only once but
who is a major figure in Fanny's later *Diary*. She observes him as
he enters the drawing room while Hetty and Susan are playing a
duet. She notes that he "stoops terribly," his mouth is always moving as if he were chewing, his fingers appear to twirl and his
hands to twist, his body continually twitches, his dress is not
suited for the occasion, and he is so near-sighted that his eye-
lashes almost touch the books on the library shelves as he inspects
the titles. At another date, Fanny states that, although Dr. Johnson "has a face the most ugly, a person the most awkward, and
manner the most singular," his "exterior" is more than compensated for by his "interior" and that "I hardly know any satisfaction
I can receive equal to listening to him." [5]

Fanny has not only a perceptive eye for people but a keen ear for their conversation. She is quick to detect unusual words or phrases, peculiar pronunciations, or distinct speech patterns. Like Boswell, she was an excellent mimic, frequently regaling members of her family and close friends with her imitations. This ability to reproduce dialogue required a discriminating ear and a retentive memory, and Fanny's sensitivity to sounds had been developed by her musical background and is attested by frequent references to how people talk. She is quick to note that *"Diable"* is a favorite expression of Signora Agujari. She records how everyone at Chessington pronounces Mlle Courvoisyois' name a different way: "Mrs. Hamilton calls her Miss *Creussy;* Mrs. Simmons, *Miss what's your name;* Mrs. Moore calls her Miss *Creusevoye;* and Kitty . . . only says Miss Crewe." [6] In writing about Omai, the South Sea native, whose fine manners and dignity charmed everyone, Fanny observed that he could pronounce "the *th* as in *thank you,* and the *w,* as in *well,* and yet cannot say the *g,* which he uses a *d* for" except in "the beginning of a word, as in *George.* . . ." [7] Whether she was reproducing the broken English of Baretti, the elegant and refined conversation of Hawkesworth, or the silly, quaint, and whimsical chatter of Kitty Cooke, Fanny's dialogue sounds realistic, natural, and faithful.

Usually she reproduces discussions at great length as if she had tape-recorded them. At times her ability to recall a lengthy conversation is unbelievable. A reader might be suspicious unless he had overheard present-day teenagers recount on the telephone for hours exactly what one person said to another during a preceding night's party. One of Fanny's contemporaries praised "the remarkable memory with which she narrates long conversations and minute details of facts and circumstances." [8] On one occasion, she amazes herself by recording a six-page discussion with Mr. Seaton. At its end she writes that she is "quite surprised to find how much of his conversation I have remembered, but as there was only him and myself [*sic*], it was not very difficult." [9]

One wishes at times that she had been more discriminating and less thorough. In the description of her father's Sunday night concert for Prince Orloff of Russia, Fanny recounts the responses of each guest to the singing of Gabrielli the previous evening. [10] The varied reactions, the comparisons with the opera star Agujari, and the speculations about the singer's health continue for six or seven pages; but only a few are devoted to the Prince, who was reputed to have been one of Catherine the Great's favorites and the murderer of Peter III. In fairness, however, one should make some allowance for the nature of the *Early Diary*. It naturally focuses on people and events interesting to Fanny and her family, who were absorbed in the world of music. Such lengthy references about singers and other musical performers are of little interest to readers today although the discussions are amusing because of Fanny's artistry in recording them, and in perceiving which people had something to say and which had said something merely to gain attention.

Most of the scenes in the *Early Diary* are not outdated. One of the most amusing is Fanny's visit at Gloucester with the flirtatious Mrs. Wall, who spends all day at her toilette, and with her "queerly droll" husband, whose amorous attentions both flattered and embarrassed Fanny. On another occasion when the Burney children were putting on an amateur production of Arthur Murphy's *The Way to Keep Him* and Henry Fielding's *Tom Thumb*, Fanny describes how they spoke and acted in many scenes, how the audience responded, how her seven-year-old niece Nancy handled the role of Tom Thumb, and how she herself changed from a highly nervous, inarticulate, stumbling actress in the early acts to a poised one, fully in command of herself.

III   The Early Diary: *Dramatic Quality*

Fanny's account of the plays exemplifies well another of her talents: the ability to present material dramatically. As Chauncey Tinker points out, Boswell is so concerned with literal truth that he does not "write up" a scene. He depends on the Johnsonian pronouncement, a trenchant utterance climaxing a short anecdote.[11] In contrast, Fanny slowly builds a rising action that vividly presents a scene with minor and major characters interacting until the situation is resolved. The previously mentioned description of the amateur production and of Fanny's gradual mastery of the part is a case in point. Another of several that might be cited is the account of Mr. Barlow's love for her, and her anxiety about being forced to marry him.

Fanny begins this episode with a brief account of an evening at her uncle's house during which she is introduced to Mr. Barlow, a short, handsome, good-tempered, and sensible young man whose language is "stiff and uncommon, and seems laboured, if not affected." [12] Practically no conversation is reproduced in this quickly delineated opening scene which ends dramatically as Mr. Barlow unexpectedly kisses Fanny good-night after her grandmother and aunts had done so. Four days later Fanny receives a letter from him.

No Richardsonian character could have penned a more artificial, flowery, and stilted epistle. After begging pardon for his liberty in writing, Mr. Barlow pays a "Tythe of Justice to the amiable lady" for the pleasant evening that gave him "such a latent Spring of Happiness." Although fearful of being accused of "Adulation," he has taken "Truth in her plainest Attire" as his guide in declaring that "The Affability, Sweetness, and Sensibility, which shone in your every Action, led me irresistably to Love and Admire the Mistress of them. . . ." Mr. Barlow concludes by requesting a meeting with Fanny and her family.

The reactions to the letter intensify the conflict. Fanny's mind is clear: she does not want to be rude to Mr. Barlow, but she is completely uninterested in him. She writes him a letter expressing appreciation for his sentiments but suggesting that he transfer them to someone else. Before sending it, she consults her father. At first he urges her to point out to Mr. Barlow that they have just met, but Fanny becomes upset at this suggestion because such a letter implies that "a longer acquaintance might be acceptable." Then Dr. Burney suggests that she send no answer; Fanny also opposes this idea because it would be treating Mr. Barlow with contempt. Still undecided about what to do, Fanny is disturbed by her grandmother and maiden aunts, who speak highly of Mr. Barlow and humorously warn her against spinsterhood. Hetty and Mr. Crisp also urge her not to dismiss her suitor lightly. The latter, particularly concerned about practical matters, points out to the dowerless girl that "this is not a marrying age, without a handsome Fortune!" He wants her to realize that, if she loses her father, she would be "an unprotected, unprovided woman." He implores her "for God's sake and your own sake, give him [Mr. Barlow] and yourself fair play . . . don't avoid seeing him."

Unable to bring herself to see Mr. Barlow or to refuse seeing him, Fanny invents a cold to excuse her absence from his evening visit. At breakfast the following morning, Mr. Barlow unexpectedly appears. His nervousness is matched by Fanny's. While she turns scarlet, he bows several times and mumbles something inco-

herently about her cold. Fortunately, Mrs. Burney and Susan take
over the conversation and ease the situation for the distressed
young man and the nonplussed Fanny, troubled not only by Mr.
Barlow's presence but also by his possibly discovering that she is
not ill.

The romance thus far described might easily have appeared in
the pages of an eighteenth-century novel. The characters are
clearly drawn, and the central conflict is firmly established. The
point of view is that of the protagonist, who finds herself torn
between her own inclinations and the advice and urgings of
friends and family. It is not unlike the opening situation in Richardson's *Clarissa,* when the heroine, although wealthy, is urged to
marry Mr. Solmes.

The short episodes that follow develop and deepen the conflict. Fanny appears at her aunt's one afternoon for tea only to
discover that Mr. Barlow has also been invited. A few days later
she receives another letter from him with language not so "high
flown" as that of the first but with similar professions of admiration and love. He hopes that his "guardian Genius" will inspire
him so that he can become "not unworthy the Esteem of your
amiable Self, and not unworthy———but stop, oh *arduous Pen,
and presume not. . . ."*

A frantic Fanny suggests to her father that she end the affair
immediately by writing a firm reply. He withholds his permission,
causing her to experience "a kind of panic" at the thought that he
favors her marriage to the young man. The climax is reached the
following afternoon when Mr. Barlow pays a surprise visit. Left
alone in the front parlor, the two converse at length. Fanny's
treatment of this key scene is masterful. By selecting only the
more revealing statements and replies and by representing the
other remarks by indirect discourse and summary, she reproduces
the entire conversation with its give and take, its extraneous remarks, its moments of painful silence, its interruptions, and its
development until Mr. Barlow gradually and reluctantly realizes
that neither now nor in the future will Fanny love him. Few
scenes in Jane Austen's superb novels are presented as vividly and
as effectively as this one between the shy, confused, enamored
swain and the courteous but firm and uninterested young lady.
While recounting it in her diary, Fanny almost never violates verisimilitude by permitting her reader to realize the time lapse be-

tween the occurrence and the writing of it. Here as elsewhere she sets the event down as it happens rather than spoil it with insights or reflections realized later.

The Barlow incident is only one of the high points in the *Early Diary*. Most of them concern Fanny herself in contrast with the more interesting sections of the later *Diary* that dwell on others. The protagonist of the *Early Diary* is a shy, perceptive, not unattractive, happy young girl, who finds herself surrounded with gay, laughing brothers, sisters, and cousins; a busy but affectionate father; an admiring "Daddy" Crisp; and gracious, friendly visitors. Whatever did not fit into this picture of pleasant domestic life was excluded from the original journal or excised from it later.

The major deletion is any unfavorable mention of the Burney's stepmother, the former Mrs. Allen. Only between the lines can readers perceive the feelings towards her. On one occasion when "The Lady," as they called the second Mrs. Burney, was away, Fanny writes that she and Susan are keeping house for their father and that they are "so happy! for he is so kind." Other remarks like this one, along with inimical statements about Mrs. Burney in unpublished material left by Fanny and the other children, suggest some of the tension in the household.[13] This situation is easy to understand because Mrs. Burney, besides being caught in the difficult stepmother role, was probably somewhat jealous of the girls for spending countless evening hours as amanuenses alone with her husband, and for sharing his interest in music, for which she cared little.

Missing from the *Early Diary* also is any mention of Fanny's stepsister Bessy, who eloped in Paris with the disreputable Mr. Meeke. Omitted too is an account of her brother Charles' expulsion from Cambridge for stealing library books. This incident, resulting in his being banished from home, was too painful and embarrassing for Fanny to perpetuate in print.[14] After a year of family discussion and deliberation, Charles was forgiven and allowed to return, but not a word to this effect appears in print. Scandal, shame, and secrets were not for the public eye.

IV *Portrait of a Young Girl*

Although Fanny's sisters, Hetty, Susan, and Charlotte, were more attractive and more musically talented than she, Fanny appears free of jealousy. Hetty and Susan were sent away to school in Paris, but their preferential treatment did not seem to affect her relationship with them or her own outlook. In part, her diffidence and modesty stemmed from her originally being considered one of the less able children. Nicknamed "The Old Lady" because of her reserve and grave composure before strangers, Fanny was especially thrilled with the attentions of older gentlemen, such as Mr. Seaton or Mr. Crispen, who perceived her keen mind and mature wit. Most people, however, preferred the talented, gregarious, laughing sisters to the silent, shy, inhibited Fanny.

Not envious, jealous, or discontented, Fanny enjoyed nearly everything she did and everyone she met. In contrast to her outward demeanor, her writing sparkles; and readers respond with delight to her youthful exuberance and enthusiasm. She reaches her peak in describing Agujari to Mr. Crisp: "She has every thing! —every requisite to accomplish a singer, in every style and manner!—the sublime and the beautiful equally at command! . . . O that you could come and hear her! Is it impossible? I die to have you enjoy the greatest luxury the world can offer;—such to me—such I am sure, to you, would be the singing of Agujari!" [15]

Crisp encouraged Fanny's naturalness and freshness; constantly he warned her that the worst fault in letter-writing is formality. He urged her "to dash away whatever comes uppermost; and believe me you'll succeed better, than by leaning on your elbows, and studying what to say." [16] When Fanny once regretted that she could find only trifles to write about, Crisp replied that he would have more of them, that such matters in letter-writing are the "very soul of genius and ease," and that he preferred candid, uninhibited letters to "fine-labour'd compositions that smelt of *the lamp*." [17] He greedily devoured whatever she wrote, complained about not hearing frequently, and berated her occasionally for not writing at greater length.

Fanny followed Crisp's advice. The *Early Diary* reads in many places like the spontaneous conversation of a spirited, vivacious teenager. Her device of addressing a Miss Nobody, much as someone would write "Dear Diary," permitted her to adopt a playful, friendly, personal tone. She might begin: "Is Nobody surprised at the date of this?—Ah, my good and excellent friend, when I last addressed myself to you from fair London town, I very little imagined that my *next* address would be from Lynn!" [18] Later Miss Nobody disappeared when Fanny's *Early Diary* consisted less of personal entries but more of journals or letters; but her refreshingly spontaneous style remained.

Much of this style is evident in her comments about books, which she read avidly. A list of her reading is broad and varied: Goldsmith's *Vicar of Wakefield,* the *Iliad* and *Odyssey,* Hume's *History of England,* Thucydides, Sterne's *Sentimental Journey* (three times), Middleton's *History of Cicero,* Dryden's translation of *Plutarch's Lives,* Voltaire's *Henriade,* Marivaux's *Vie de Marianne,* Stanyan's *Grecian History,* and Johnson's *Rasselas,* among others. On the whole, Fanny reveals little critical perception but a taste for sentimentality and morality. She disliked the way that Goldsmith's *Vicar* referred to his wife; but, as she proceeded, she enjoyed the "rural felicity," the "simple, unaffected contentment," and "family domestic happiness." She wrote that "before I was half thro' the first volume, I was, as I may truly express myself, *surprised into tears*—and in the second volume, I really sobb'd." [19]

Yet Fanny is capable of sound literary criticism as exemplified by her disparagement of Mrs. Rowe's *Letters from the Dead to the Living:* "They are so very enthusiastick, that the religion she preaches rather disgusts and cloys than charms and elevates—and so romantick, that every word betrays improbability, instead of disguising fiction, and displays the author, instead of human nature. For my own part, I cannot be much pleased without an appearance of truth; at least of possibility—I wish the story to be natural tho' the sentiments are refined; and the characters to be probable tho' their behavior is excelling." [20]

Fanny's zest for books was more than matched by her predilection for people. Naturally, the ones attracting most of her attention were the celebrities attending the informal Sunday evening concerts in her father's home. Since most of these individuals have faded away into general oblivion, few others besides eighteenth-century specialists recognize such "lyons" as James Bruce, the enormous African explorer; Reverend Thomas Twining, the Classical scholar; Dr. John Armstrong, poet and physician; Miss Elza Linley (afterwards Mrs. Sheridan), the beautiful singer; Dr. Shebbeare, the ill-mannered novelist; Dr. John Hawkesworth, author, editor, and translator; Millico, Sacchini, Agujari, and Gabrielli, the magnificent Italian singers; and the previously mentioned Omai and Prince Orloff.

Of all the father's London friends and acquaintances, David
Garrick held the warmest place in Fanny's heart. To her and to
the other young Burneys, no one was so much fun. He adored
playing with the children so much that Fanny pitied his own lack
of them. She found it impossible to capture "this most entertaining of mortals" in her journal because so much of "his drollery
belongs to his voice, looks, and manner." [21] Despite this statement,
Donald Stauffer asserts that the young Fanny surpassed two of
Garrick's contemporary biographers, Arthur Murphy and Thomas
Davies, in portraying him.[22] Her picture of the great Roscius is not
limited to his pranks, jokes, and buffoonery in the Burney home.
She admires him in many stage roles. As Abel Drugger in Johnson's *Alchemist,* he amazes her: "Never could I have imagined
such a metamorphose [*sic*] as I saw; the extreme meanness, the
vulgarity, the low wit, the vacancy of countenance, the appearance of *unlicked nature* in all his motions. In short, never was
character so well entered into, yet so opposite to his own." [23]

The greatest praise was reserved for Garrick as Richard III:
"Garrick was sublimely horrible! Good Heavens—how he made
me shudder whenever he appeared! It is inconceivable how terribly great he is in this character! I will never see him so disfig-
ured again; he seemed so truly the monster he performed, that I
felt myself glow with indignation every time I saw him." [24] She
was not alone in her panegyric because the applause that evening
was so thunderous that the seats shook and the theater was almost
torn down.

Fanny's interest in people did not extend to servants, shopkeepers, tradesmen, farmers, artisans, carriage drivers, or other members of the lower-middle and lower classes. John, the Burney's
servant, is mentioned only once, and then in passing. Fanny came
in contact with numerous people from different classes and occu-
pational groups as her novels disclose, but she evidently accepted
the social discrimination of her day and excluded such individuals
from her personal letters and journals.

Also omitted from the *Early Diary* is any mention of political
events. There is not a word about John Wilkes, the Boston Tea
Party, the Royal Marriage Act, the American Revolution, or other
matters during the hectic years before William Pitt the Younger,
the great prime minister, brought economic and political stability
to a floundering government. Women were not supposed to be

interested in or able to understand these affairs, and Fanny was no exception.

Fanny describes, however, various social activities that she watched or participated in. While visiting her married stepsister, Maria Allen Rishton, one summer at the seashore town of Teignmouth, she writes about the races, the cricket match, the wrestling contest, the rowing match, and the net fishing by the women. At home in London, she fills her journal with accounts of concerts, masquerades, *conversaziones,* plays, and weddings. Yet in all of these there is a lack of descriptive detail. Only on special occasions does she notice dress. Rarely does she mention furniture, food, jewelry, homes, grounds, carriages, or anything material. Money was a constant worry for her father; lack of luxuries does not seem to have disturbed the young Fanny. That she desired little, expected little, and was satisfied with little contributed much to her later happiness in life.

In no way did nature appear to compensate for material wants; in fact, Fanny preferred the city to the country. Although she is always happy to be at Chessington Hall with Mr. Crisp, it is mainly due to his presence and the absence of her stepmother. She never writes about enjoying the countryside, the flowers, a sunset, or a star-studded sky. What she emphatically dislikes about country life is having to be pleasant and agreeable to everyone, and having to visit back and forth. She protests being forced to waste her time one summer at King's Lynn with "such a set of tittle tattle, prittle prattle visitants" and complains about "the ceremony and fuss of these fall lall people." In London she can "decline as well as accept" visitors and invitations. At sixteen she is certain that she could live only in a city or a large village because a town "has all the bad qualities, without one of the good ones, of both." [25] Fanny's desire to select her friends and acquaintances and to be free from social protocol created the greatest problem for her when she later became part of the confining royal household.

V *Growth of an Author*

While the *Early Diary* sheds light on eighteenth-century English society as observed by a perceptive, bright young girl from her vantage point in an unusual family with numerous literary, musical, scholarly, and theatrical friends, the main focus of the

Early Diary is on Fanny herself. Its pages serve as a preface to *Evelina,* whose publication provides a fitting climax. To read the *Early Diary* is to discover not only what it was like to be a young girl in eighteenth-century London mingling with artistic and fashionable people but also how an embryonic novelist grew up and developed into a literary figure.

Since Fanny began her diary in 1768, her father had received a doctorate of music at Oxford College and had published three books—*The Present State of Music in France and Italy; The Present State of Music in Germany, the Netherlands, and the United Provinces;* and the first volume of his major work, *The General History of Music*—as well as other miscellaneous pieces. Influenced strongly by him, Fanny also turned to writing. Whether in the Cabin or Look Out in the garden at King's Lynn, in Maria's cottage at Teignmouth, or in the playroom or observatory (where Sir Isaac Newton had worked), Fanny enjoyed scribbling away in her diary or in letters to Mr. Crisp. She looked forward to writing in the afternoons and evenings after laboring at needlework in the mornings. "The pleasure of popping down" her thoughts she found to be "irresistible."

This delight undoubtedly stemmed in part from the profuse praises lavished upon her by Mr. Crisp. He enjoyed her letters personally but in addition, as a literary person, he realized the value of her picture of manners, indicating that "if specimens of this kind had been preserved of the different *Tons* that have succeeded one another for twenty centuries past, how interesting would they have been." He asked her to send "more, and more." [26]

At this time Fanny was surreptitiously writing *Evelina.* Disapproving of novels, Mrs. Burney was responsible for Fanny's burning her first work, *The History of Caroline Evelyn;* the second one, therefore, had to be concealed. But a greater obstacle was Fanny's lack of time. Serving as her father's copyist, Fanny toiled tirelessly while he worked late after teaching students from seven in the morning to nine at night, or while he dictated to her from his bed when crippled with rheumatism or plagued by other illnesses. Yet Fanny gained a great deal from her experience as his amanuensis. Lacking any formal education, she developed a sense of style and an ear for language by working with her father. Crisp refers to this advantage when he writes, "You have learned from that Rogue your father (by so long serving as amanuensis, I suppose) to make your descriptions alive." [27] In addition, Dr. Burney served as an inspiring example by his assiduous efforts to write regardless of time, place, or health. He labored incessantly, seizing odd moments, taking advantage of cancelled appointments, working on Sundays and holidays, and staying awake until the morning hours. Nearly all of Fanny's books were written under similarly trying conditions.

By the winter of 1776, nine years after she had started her second novel, Fanny had completed two volumes of *Evelina* and had outlined a third. She set about copying the volumes in a disguised hand to insure that her writing would not be recognized from her work on Dr. Burney's manuscripts. *Evelina* had to be published anonymously to avoid antagonizing Mrs. Burney, to protect her father's reputation, and to evade the odium of being known as a novelist.

Fanny's brother, cousin, and sisters selected a publisher, Dodsley, with her, sent him a letter, and awaited the reply. After he had refused, Lowndes indicated his willingness to read the two volumes. Charles, carefully disguised, carried the manuscript one night to Lowndes' office. In a few days the publisher, replying to a coffeehouse address, agreed to print the novel when it was finished. Fanny was disappointed at this delay; but, by resolutely setting to work, she soon completed the third volume and revised the first two. In so doing, as Hemlow shows,[28] she made the language more elegant and dignified. Much of the fresh, natural, colloquial style of her *Early Diary*, highly praised by Crisp, was corrected and polished. It was as if Fanny, realizing that *Evelina* would appear in print, worried about the novel's being disparaged by critics and fashionable people.

The story of the reception accorded *Evelina* and its author is mainly treated in Fanny's *Diary*. In it she sketches somewhat self-consciously her ensuing rise from obscurity to renown. Her *Early Diary* tells of the self-education and development of a modest, carefree girl who enjoys life and people, and who writes with wit, insight, and vitality in a refreshing and natural manner. Although lacking the plot, suspense, unity, and other fictional ingredients of *Evelina*, Fanny's *Early Diary* is just as charming, delightful, and fascinating.

CHAPTER 2

A Young Lady's Entrance into the World

"THERE ought to be a book, of laws and customs, *a-la-mode*, presented to all young people upon their first introduction into public company." [1] This statement by the heroine of *Evelina* suggests one of Fanny's aims in writing the novel and its special appeal for "the young ladies" and "boarding-school damsels," who, according to its preface, were incurable of the novel-reading "distemper" but who might read this work, "if not with advantage, at least without injury." *Evelina* allowed these readers to experience vicariously the life of a seventeen-year-old middle-class country girl in gay London. There she suffered embarrassment and humiliation because of her inexperience and indiscretion, her uncertain parentage, and her association with vulgar relatives. Feminine readers could more easily identify with the innocent, unsophisticated Evelina than with rape-prone Pamela, the saintly Clarissa, the courageous Sophia, the heroic Amelia, or the foolhardy Betsy Thoughtless. [2]

Moreover, *Evelina* embodied four surefire plot elements: (1) the plight of an abandoned child; (2) the entrance of a young girl into social life; (3) the misfortunes of a country girl in the big city; and (4) the romance of a Cinderella with a Prince Charming. In addition, Fanny provided readers with a work of moral instruction, a guide to fashionable London places, a picture of contemporary manners and morals, satirical portraits of middle and upper class characters, and scenes of boisterous farce and touching sentimentality.

Happily for present readers, *Evelina*'s farfetched plot and intrusive didacticism do not obscure the book's merit. Fanny is concerned more with people than with action. She is at her best in exposing characters rather than working out ideas. Her bent is for comedy rather than philosophy. Her forte is revealing the affectations, vices, and follies of people as they interact with one an-

other. To bring a wide variety of characters together, Fanny constructed an elaborate plot; most of the complicated events, however, occur before the novel commences. Even though the
background of the story is intricate, the action is simple, clear, and
direct.

I *The Unified Plot*

Evelina is a continuation of *The History of Caroline Evelyn,*
Fanny's juvenile novel destroyed in the bonfire. This work dealt
with the unfortunate marriage of wealthy Mr. Evelyn to a tavern
girl, the birth of their daughter Caroline, the death soon afterwards of Mr. Evelyn, and the rearing of the child by his friend
and tutor, Mr. Villars. According to the terms of Mr. Evelyn's will,
Caroline at eighteen went to live in Paris with her mother, then
married to Monsieur Duval. To avoid marrying Duval's nephew,
Caroline ran away and privately married Sir John Belmont, a
profligate young man. When he destroyed their marriage certifi-
cate and deserted her, Caroline returned to Mr. Villars, died, and
left him her child Evelina.

Fanny's second novel, *Evelina,* starts seventeen years later
when Mr. Villars allows his ward to accompany Mrs. Mirvan and
her daughter to London to see something of life there and to meet
Captain Mirvan, who is returning from a voyage. The heroine enjoys the theater, places of amusement, and the opera but suffers at
several dances for her contretemps with the foppish Mr. Lovel
and the rakish Sir Clement Willoughby, and for revealing her social awkwardness and lack of sophistication with the handsome
Lord Orville. In London she also meets by coincidence her maternal grandmother, Madame Duval, who introduces Evelina to the
Branghtons, her cousins.

After a short sojourn in the country, Evelina visits Madame Duval in London. Living with her grandmother in the middle-class
Holborn district and associating with the Branghtons in their
shabby Snow Hill rooms, Evelina sees the bourgeois side of life.
The satire is devastating in this section of the novel as Fanny ruth-
lessly exposes the vulgarity, coarseness, and tactlessness of the
Branghtons and their friend, the conceited city beau, Mr. Smith.

Plot complexities develop when Lord Orville encounters Evelina in awkward situations with her vulgar relatives. Her life is
also complicated by an impoverished poet, Macartney, whom

Evelina saves from committing suicide. He had fallen in love with
a girl that he has since discovered to be his sister, and he had
almost killed her father whom he now knows to be his own. This
sentimental subplot with its elements of incest and patricide is not
uncommon in eighteenth-century fiction.

With Evelina's fortunes at their nadir because of her father's
refusal to acknowledge her as his daughter, Madame Duval's annoyance with her, and Lord Orville's insult to her, she broods in
despair. Mr. Villars' advice provides little solace; a change of
scenery is recommended. Accompanied by a family friend, Mrs.
Selwyn, the depressed Evelina goes to a spa, Bristol Hotwells.
Here she regains her health not by taking the baths but by clarify-
ing numerous misunderstandings with Lord Orville, learning that
Sir Clement had forged Orville's name to an insulting letter, discovering that Macartney is her brother, and convincing a repen-
tant Sir John Belmont that she is truly his daughter. All ends well
with Evelina, now Lady Belmont, becoming Countess Orville.

This plot review does not suggest *Evelina*'s variety, tight construction, and dependence upon coincidence. Fanny constantly al-
ternates the serious with the satirical, the country with the city,
the upper class with the middle class, the sentimental with the
farcical, and the didactic with the frivolous. Near the end, for
example, is an emotionally saturated reconciliation scene between
Evelina and her father. Filled with remorse, Sir John Belmont is
overcome at the sight of his daughter, who, in the grand gesture
typical of eighteenth-century heroines, kneels before him, refuses
to accept his apologies, and implores him not to reproach himself.
Choking with tears and sighs, he blesses her and hastens away;
she is left "almost drowned in tears." Readers of the period took
special pleasure in such mawkish orgies.

Almost immediately afterwards, Fanny breaks the mood by
having Captain Mirvan introduce a fashionably dressed monkey
as one of Mr. Lovel's relatives. Like an earlier practical joke on
Madame Duval, this one provides some amusement but is pro-
longed so much that the comedy wears off and sympathy for the
victim sets in. Nevertheless, Fanny has succeeded in snapping
short the sentimentality of the previous scene.

Evelina's unified construction may be realized from the fact
that nearly all the characters are essential to the plot. Macartney,
apparently inserted for the sentimental subplot, is vital in reveal-

ing Evelina's courage, in serving as an impediment in her romance, and in solving the sticky problem of Polly Green in the
denouement. This young lady, the child of Carolyn Evelyn's maid,
is reared and educated as Lady Belmont by Sir John in the belief
that she is his daughter. Upon discovering the deception, he is
faced with the problem of exposing and hurting the unknowing,
innocent girl. Macartney, the son of another woman whom Sir
John had married and deserted, is eager to wed Polly, whom he
had loved in Paris before learning that she was his sister. Now
that she is not related to him, Macartney makes her Lady Belmont
by marriage, thereby restoring the title she had just lost when
Evelina replaced her as Sir John Belmont's daughter. Thus Fanny
provides for what might have been an annoying loose plot end.

Even the minor characters play vital roles. Mrs. Clinton, Evelina's former nurse and currently Villars' housekeeper, is mentioned sporadically early in the novel. At the end she identifies
Dame Green (Polly's mother and Evelina's first nurse) and makes
her confess how she deceived Sir John. Another minor character,
Monsieur Du Bois, Madame Duval's escort, functions both as a
comic figure due to his ignorance of English, and as a decoy in the
practical joke played on Madame Duval; later, as a young man
romantically interested in Evelina, he causes the jealous grandmother to return the girl to Mr. Villars. This separation from
Madame Duval allows Evelina to gain admission to the fashionable society in Bristol Hotwells through her new companion, Mrs.
Selwyn.

While Fanny has worked out her plot carefully by utilizing
most of the characters to further the action, she has relied heavily
on chance and coincidence. Lord Orville is ubiquitous, appearing almost wherever Evelina goes, especially when his presence
would be most awkward. Sir Clement also has the knack of turning up at inappropriate times, and once he is conveniently able to
intercept her letter to the hero. Evelina's accidental meetings with
Madame Duval in London and with Macartney, later revealed as
her brother, are other improbable incidents. For that matter, the
entire Macartney subplot is incredible, as is the substitution of
the baby Polly Green for Evelina, an occurrence not usual in early
fiction. Fanny adds a new touch to the resolution of the child-
switching. Unable to have her heroine conveniently reveal a
strawberry mark by baring her chest or back, Fanny bases the

recognition scene on Evelina's close resemblance to her mother. As soon as he sees the heroine, Sir John Belmont knows that she is Caroline Evelyn's daughter.

II *The Use of Letters*

Because Fanny's story is incidental to her picture of manners, the reader forgives her for depending on coincidence just as he does Fielding in *Tom Jones*. Looking instead at her handling of the epistolary form, one realizes her artistry. She generally avoids the main pitfalls: having Evelina write under impossible conditions or describe incidents that she normally could not have witnessed. Evelina's letters about the evening's or day's events are composed the following morning. Unlike Pamela, she writes neither while being raped nor while running away. Like Pamela, she is the central figure, directly involved in every episode and with every character. She candidly relates all experiences to her beloved guardian, Mr. Villars; but she is reticent about her growing love for Lord Orville. No reader is unaware of her romantic interest, however.

In several incidents Fanny strains for credibility against the rigid restrictions of epistolary form. The first involves her describing the practical joke that Captain Mirvan and Sir Clement play on Madame Duval. To write vividly about the episode, she must see it. To do so, however, she must either be aware that Captain Duval and Sir Clement are disguised as robbers or not. If the latter, then readers, viewing events through her eyes, may miss the humor. But, if Evelina knows that the robbers are impostors, then why does this sweet girl acquiesce in this heartless plan? Fanny resolves the dilemma by having the aware Evelina on the verge of exposing the hoax several times but deciding against it on each occasion because of the Captain's probable anger towards her or because of Madame Duval's inevitable fury towards the Captain. Furthermore, Evelina later declares that she would have revealed everything if she had known that the Captain was going to leave Madame Duval bruised and terrified in a muddy ditch. The excuse is flimsy, but it is necessary to permit Evelina's eyewitness account.

Fanny is hard put to give credibility to her heroine's later actions. Evelina, seeing a gun revealed when Macartney stumbles, realizes that he may commit suicide. She follows him to his room, hears him ask God's forgiveness, rushes in, stops him from killing himself, faints, quickly revives, pleads with him, takes his pistols, returns to her room, and collapses. Such improbable fainting and sudden recovery are necessary if the eighteenth-century heroine must see what occurs and prevent Macartney's suicide.

In these two instances Fanny has Evelina describe the events. On two other occasions Evelina obtains vital information in an unlikely manner from others. Lord Orville and Mr. Lovel comment on her bad manners in dancing with the former after refusing the latter. Lord Orville also disparages her for being unable to discuss any of the many subjects that he had raised. It is highly doubtful that Maria Mirvan, Evelina's close friend, would have overheard this conversation; but, even if she had, she certainly would have been discreet enough not to repeat it to the sensitive heroine. Yet Fanny wanted "the boarding school damsels" to learn the lesson in manners, and to realize the extent of Evelina's *faux pas* as well as to account for Lord Orville's coolness towards her.

Another awkward situation due to the epistolary form arises when Sir Clement forcibly detains Evelina in Mrs. Beaumont's garden. Hearing her cries, Lord Orville comes to her aid. Evelina flees into the house, frightened at her near escape and alarmed that the two men might quarrel violently. Fanny's problem at this point is how to describe the dramatic scene between the two men with Evelina absent. The author solves it by sending Mrs. Selwyn to the garden; there, without being observed, she conveniently hears Lord Orville declare his love for Evelina.

Two other difficulties arise from Fanny's use of the epistolary form. The first she handles well. Evelina must have a confidant to whom she can write about her adventures and her feelings. Mr. Villars serves this function when Evelina lives away from him. When she is with him, however, a difficulty might have arisen if Fanny had not provided another confidant, Maria Mirvan. That this character exists solely for this purpose and is not a person in her own right may be adduced from the innocuous role she plays, from her failure to write Fanny any letters, and from her lack of romantic involvement. The creation of Maria is another example of Fanny's skillful plotting.

But another stylistic matter is handled inconsistently. Since Evelina writes about past events, she is aware of their outcome. One expects, therefore, that the opening sentences of her letters will foreshadow what follows. Usually Fanny provides the appropriate signals. One letter, for example, begins: "O my dear Sir, I now write in the greatest uneasiness! Mme. Duval has made me a proposal which terrifies me to death, and which was as unexpected as it was shocking." [3] Sometimes, however, Evelina begins with little suggestion of the following dramatic events. The letter describing Sir Clement's terrifying abduction attempt commences with the prosaic statement that she has "a volume to write, of the adventures of yesterday." [4] Evelina also recounts Lord Orville's startling marital proposal with a similarly casual introduction.[5]

The novel would have profited by the novelty and variety resulting from letters by the comic characters, as did Smollett's *Humphrey Clinker*. Certainly Madame Duval, the Branghtons, and Mr. Smith could have penned hilarious pieces. But this criticism does not imply that Fanny fails to sustain interest by restricting the letter-writing. On the contrary, the great bulk of the letters, those by Evelina, are as highly enjoyable as Fanny's are in the *Early Diary*. Nearly all are fresh, natural, ebullient, vivid, and consistent with the character of a young girl reacting to new places, people, and experiences.

Particularly delightful are the letters prior to and during Evelina's initial London visit. In one, for example, Evelina writes to Mr. Villars about whether to accompany the Mirvans to London or not. After explaining the circumstances, she politely asks for his advice but, in order not to influence him, states that she will not be disappointed if he refuses to grant her permission. As she continues, her feelings become apparent. She mentions that the London season has begun: "two playhouses are open,—the Opera-house,—Ranelagh, and the Pantheon." Once again she expresses her indifference about going, but her words belie her: "Don't suppose I make any point of going, for I shall hardly sigh, to see them depart without me, though I shall probably never meet with such another opportunity." Finally, the seventeen-year-old girl cannot contain herself longer: "I believe I am bewitched! I made a resolution, when I began, that I would not be urgent; but my pen—or rather my thoughts, will not suffer me to keep it—for I acknowledge, I must acknowledge, I cannot help wishing for your permission." [6]

In London, Evelina sounds like Fanny of the *Early Diary* in her partiality for the opera, and her enthusiastic response to Garrick

("such ease! such vivacity in his manner! such grace in his motions! such fire and meaning in his eyes!").[7] She is everywhere
the adolescent awakening to a new world. Typically, she has
"hardly time to breathe." She cannot get accustomed to men is
expressing appreciation to her for honoring them with a dance
("O these fashionable people!"). She is dazzled by the famous
places (Ranelagh is like "some enchanted castle or fairy palace").
Evelina is the prototype of the young country girl going to the
large sophisticated city, whether it be London, Paris, or New York,
in the eighteenth, nineteenth, or twentieth centuries.

In contrast to Evelina's letters, Mr. Villars' are formal, ponderous, stilted, and sententious. As Will Hale points out, he writes
Johnsonese.[8] Certainly those who blame the great Cham for
Fanny's later stylistic deterioration have not read Mr. Villars' letters or the preface to *Evelina*.[9] Yet within the context of the
novel, the mentor's grand style serves as an effective contrast to
the informal one of the young girl.

III *The Characters*

One wishes that Fanny had been able to humanize Mr. Villars
and Lord Orville. But, just as Fielding and Richardson were unable to make Allworthy and Grandison lifelike, so Fanny does not
succeed with her mentor and paragon characters. Both these men
speak the artificial language of the courtesy books and the sentimental novels. That Fanny even fails to distinguish between the
two men is evident from the similarity of their names (note also
the *ville*[10] in Evelina Anville), from the heroine's frequent comparison of them, and from her blind obedience to both. When
Lord Orville mentions the impropriety of her meeting Macartney,
Evelina breaks her engagement with the poor poet rather than
risk the paragon's disfavor. Similarly, when Mr. Villars tells her
to leave Lord Orville immediately because her love will not be returned, she readily acquiesces without a murmur. This prompt
and blind compliance from the spirited young girl has been condi-
tioned by the teacher-like roles of both men. Theirs are the voices
of Experience speaking Truth. The novel is replete with such advice as the following: "Remember, my dear Evelina, nothing is so
delicate as the reputation of a woman; it is at once the most beautiful and most brittle of all human things." [11]

Although both men proffer instruction about proper social con-

duct, generally Mr. Villars functions as a counselor while Lord
Orville serves as a model. Yet in one important instance the latter
falls short by proposing to Evelina without inquiring about her
"family and connections," particularly about the "low" people
often with her. Fanny tries to excuse his oversight by having him
claim to be afraid of never seeing Evelina again and to having "a
partiality that has known no bounds." Such impetuous action,
however, does not befit the eighteenth-century paragon.

Although both Mr. Villars and Lord Orville are key figures in
the plot, they do not play major roles as individual characters. Mr.
Villars' letters, many of them short, total only fifteen of the novel's
eighty-four. Never does he meet any of the other characters, and
never are readers informed about his present or former life, except
his being a tutor to Mr. Evelyn and guardian to Caroline Evelyn.
Mr. Villars serves only as a functional character to receive Evelina's candid letters and to proffer moral observations and wise
advice for the benefit of the heroine and other "Evelinas" reading
the novel.

Similarly, Lord Orville is important as a functional character
rather than as a person. As the paragon, he provides the male love
interest, and is attracted or indifferent to Evelina according to her
decorum or lack of it. Although he appears in many early scenes,
only in the final ones does he speak to any extent. Then he is the
quintessence of wisdom and politeness, but like Grandison—a
bore. Lord Orville is characterized throughout by the epithet
"noble" ("noblest of men," "noble-minded," "noble-hearted"), a
word more suggestive of chivalrous knights than eighteenth-
century heroes. His virtues, however, are those of the age: he is
intelligent, courteous, sensitive, polite, and aristocratic. His vices
are non-existent, for he does not gamble, play cards, drink, or race
his phaeton (the sports car of its day). In addition he exudes
strength, firmness, and masculinity, being able to protect Evelina
from Mr. Lovel and Sir Clement without involving himself in a
rash duel.

Although Fanny, like most authors, is unconvincing in her portrayal of the monitor and paragon, she succeeds in delineating the
heroine. Fanny's artistry is particularly apparent in the early sections of the novel when Evelina is characterized as a giddy, unsophisticated, awkward young girl. Nowhere is she depicted so
effectively as at Mrs. Stanley's ball, where she is provoked by the

haughty stares of the sauntering gentlemen, convulsed by the ostentatious manners and foppish dress of Mr. Lovel, abashed at dancing with a nobleman, and nonplussed at the accusation of being ill-mannered. This scene portraying the range of feelings experienced by the young girl is one of the most memorable in eighteenth-century literature.

As the novel progresses, Fanny's portrayal of Evelina becomes less convincing. On the one hand, there is the naïve country girl, deceived and discredited at the balls because of her inexperience and ignorance of social customs. This is the young lady whom Mr. Villars calls "his little rustic . . . who knows nothing of the world." Lady Howard describes her as "ingenuous and simple," Mr. Lovel insists that she must be "a rustic," Madame Duval laments her "bumpkinish air," and Lord Orville, even after knowing her a while, states that she is very young and very inexperienced.

On the other hand, there is Evelina the letter-writer. This character possesses keen insight and sound judgment, proving to be anything but simple. She immediately perceives that Mr. Lovel is a fop, Captain Mirvan crude, Madame Duval coarse, Sir Clement dangerous, Lord Merton rude, the Branghtons vulgar, and Mr. Smith unrefined. No one deceives the young girl from Berry Hill.

What causes this conflict in character? The answer probably lies in Fanny's inability to detach herself from her heroine and also to handle the first person narrator ironically. Although today's readers might deplore Evelina's snobbery and hypocrisy towards Madame Duval, Mr. Smith, and the Branghtons, there is no evidence in the novel that Fanny is slyly satirizing her heroine. Indeed, at all times Evelina is presented sympathetically and attractively, often serving as a mouthpiece for the author. This identification of author-character may account in part for Fanny's failure to achieve the double vision necessary for irony. Actually the situation required a greater artist, a Jane Austen, who might have had Evelina write favorably of certain characters, and who would have made readers aware of their shortcomings. But Fanny had neither the heart nor the head for such complexities. The result is that Evelina the narrator, who judges people accurately and incisively, is far wiser than Evelina the heroine, who has spent all her life protected and secluded in the country.

Of course, after Evelina's initial indiscretions, her prudent conduct and acute perspicacity are necessary for the happy ending.

Fanny did not wish her innocent heroine to suffer tragically in the city. She planned instead to show how Evelina gained the necessary *politesse* and experience to develop into an intelligent, sophisticated young lady, one worthy of becoming the paragon's wife. But, in fact, Evelina is a static character who is little wiser at the end than in the beginning. She has learned, of course, how to refuse dance invitations tactfully. She has become more vividly aware of the danger of accepting rides from libertines like Sir Clement. She now knows better than to stroll along "the dark alleys" in Vauxhall. And she will not initiate a correspondence with a gentleman again. But besides these social conventions, she has learned little about values, morals, or people, suggesting that a social education is all. By such standards, Evelina is ready to take her place in society; by other standards, she has merely exchanged snobbery for sweetness, and sympathy for indifference.

Yet Evelina has also learned that dreams may come true. She and women readers like her have discovered that Lord Orvilles are waiting for them somewhere, waiting and willing to overlook their social faults and family background for their simple charm and innocent purity. The *Critical Review* in September, 1778, attacked the excessively happy ending by wishing that Evelina's "husband had not been a lord, and that her father had been less rich." It continued by charging that readers of such novels would become frustrated with their menial lives if they succumbed to the belief that "happiness is not to be found in the chilling climate of low life, nor even . . . in the temperate zone of middle life— Rank alone contains this unknown good, wealth alone can bestow this coveted joy."

Certainly *Evelina* is guilty of being escape literature by ending in such an implausibly happy manner but so did most eighteenth-century novels. Richardson, Fielding, Smollett, Defoe, and Goldsmith all reward the heroes and heroines in the major novels in unexpected and unbelievable ways. In this respect, Fanny's faults were those of her age.

Like most women, eighteenth-century woman loved to dream; more than most women, she loved to weep, and in this practice men joined her. Books in the second half of the century were water-soaked from the tears of readers who enjoyed not only a good cry but a constant one.[12] Novels were saturated with distressing situations, fainting heroines, affected men, and tender episodes. To today's readers, the tearful meeting between Evelina and Sir John Belmont is embarrassing, the frenetic scenes with Macartney are melodramatic, and the stilted courtship of Evelina and Lord Orville is painful.

Although containing such sentimentality, *Evelina* does not exploit emotion as did most novels of the period. The heroine does cry sometimes, and even faints upon occasion; but in her struggles against Sir Clement and in her courageous action to prevent Macartney from committing suicide, she is a far cry from the delicate, fastidious creatures swooning upon touch or at the sound of a proposal.[13] Macartney with his poetic soul, his suicidal tendencies, and his melancholy nature is in keeping with the sentimental prototype, but his role in *Evelina* is minor. The hero, Lord Orville, is not cast in this mold. He is not supercharged with emotion, pulsating with passion, or throbbing with tenderness. Nor is the tone of the novel one of high seriousness, which is essential for the somber emotions of pity and compassion. Lacking such characteristics, *Evelina* cannot be classified among the sentimental novels of the period although admittedly it is too sentimental for the taste of readers today.

IV Comedy of Manners

Evelina offers something to those reading for moral instruction, escape, and an emotional release; but primarily the novel provides an opportunity to laugh at the follies and foibles of those deviating from the accepted social norm. Fanny has a sharp eye and a keen ear; little escapes her notice. She deftly reproduces the affectations, absurdities, and eccentricities of people in the middle and upper classes. Her satirical portraits rely mainly on speech and manners rather than on physical qualities or dress. Many of the figures are caricatures in the tradition of the comedy of "humours," but others, particularly the middle-class individuals, are less simply conceived and more vividly presented.

Dr. Johnson's favorite was Mr. Smith: "Henry Fielding never drew such a character—such a fine varnish of low politeness! such a struggle to appear a gentleman! Madam, there is no character better drawn anywhere—in any book or by any author."[14] And Dr. Johnson's superlatives are justified. In Mr. Smith's own eyes, and in those of the Branghton girls, he is a fashionable gentleman, adored by the ladies, and admired by the men. He attributes his

good spirits to being single, although he implies that many
women have tried to do something about this. He even in mock
jest states that he must be careful about eating anything they offer
because he might be poisoned for being so handsome. Evelina
finds this Holborn beau to be boorish, officious, and disagreeable.
She points out that he is dressed "in a very showy manner, but
without any taste," that his attempt "to put on the fine gentleman"
was futile, and that he "objects to everything that is not proposed
by himself."

In addition to having Evelina ridicule the beau, Fanny uses the
comic device of self-exposure by having Mr. Smith reveal his ignorance after bragging about his knowledge. No sooner, for example, does he declare that he is an expert on art, than he identifies Neptune as a general in the Hayman painting at Vauxhall.

Fanny also contrasts Mr. Smith with Sir Clement. This gentleman tries to abduct Evelina in his carriage, aids Captain Mirvan
in his practical joke on Madame Duval, and falsely ingratiates
himself with the Mirvans. More concerned with manners than
morals, Fanny overlooks these faults in having her heroine state
that Sir Clement's "language . . . is always that of a gentleman;
and his address and manners are so very superior . . . that, to
make any comparison between him and Mr. Smith, would be extremely unjust." [15]

Although the snobbish Fanny prefers Sir Clement to the Holborn beau, she does not admire him. At fault is not his libertinism.
Like Richardson, Fanny does not condemn a man merely because
he resorts to foul means to seduce. Sins of affectation or vulgarity
are more heinous in Fanny's Inferno. Yet, despite his plea at the
novel's end that he was motivated "by a passion the most violent
that ever warmed the heart of man," Sir Clement fails to win Evelina's forgiveness for his falsely giving his word of honor and for
his forging Lord Orville's name. Fine manners may excuse sexual
immorality but not deceit and dishonesty.

In literature the evil or immoral characters are often conceived
more artistically and presented more interestingly than the good
or virtuous ones. In *Evelina* Sir Clement is delineated with more
skill than Lord Orville or Mr. Villars. He is cleverly tormenting to
Evelina when she lies to him about having a dance partner, perceptively witty in analyzing other characters, superbly skillful in
ingratiating himself with all types of people, and magnificently

suave in attempting to prove attractive to Evelina. Perhaps fearful
of making Sir Clement too appealing, Fanny spoils his characterization at the end by having him act the heavy villain.

Just as Sir Clement serves as a foil to Mr. Smith, so Captain
Mirvan is contrasted with Madame Duval. He deplores and
sneers at anything not English, from a puppet show to a human
being. Madame Duval abhors everything English, whether it be
the people, who are "ill-bred brutes," or the manners, which are
"barbarous." Naturally, these characters constantly squabble with
each other. Not content to confine their natures to this one "humour," Fanny adds another dimension to each. Captain Mirvan,
like Smollett's immortal nautical character, Hawser Trunnion,
talks as if he were still at sea. Evelina complains about the difficulty of transcribing his conversation because of his oaths, which
she decorously omits, and because of his sea-terms, which are un-
intelligible to her. Nevertheless, she suggests the salty flavor of his
speech. In mentioning the practical joke that he intends to play
upon Madame Duval, the Captain says, "I am now upon a hazard-
ous expedition, having undertaken to convey a crazy vessel to the
shores of Mortification." If anyone informs Madame Duval, the
Captain will look upon that individual as "mutinying" and turn
him "adrift." [10]

Fanny's characterization of Captain Mirvan is inconsistent because she evidently admired him more than the reader is led to
expect. Evelina immediately labels him "surly, vulgar, and disagreeable." He is all of these things. Obviously he does not belong
in the punctilious society of Mr. Villars, Lord Orville, and others.
Yet he is clearly preferable to Mr. Smith and the Branghtons because he lacks their pretensions and affectations. He may be ill-
mannered and uncouth, but he is honest and frank. He may be
rough around the edges, but he is good at heart. In Fanny's
scheme of social conformity, Captain Mirvan wins some respect
and admiration for his candor and his hatred of sham and hypocrisy; but he remains a social outcast. Fanny had a spot for the
crude individualist in her heart but not in her society.

Madame Duval is a fine counterpart for the Captain. Her
speech with its characteristic "ma Foi's," double and even triple
negatives, and compound superlatives ("most impudentest") is as
distinctive and colorful as his nautical talk. Equally fascinating is
her explosive wrath when pushed in the mud or manhandled. The

recipient of a pie in the face or the butt of any practical joke on
stage or in fiction should not be apathetic or deserving of sympathy, and Madame Duval is neither. She is too coarse, affected, and
aggressive to be pitied; she is too volatile, outspoken, and emotional to be complacent. Consequently, she is the perfect target
for the Captain's jokes.

Among Fanny's best conceived characters are the Branghtons:
Mr. Branghton, his son Tom, and his daughters Biddy and Polly.
This ill-mannered, insensitive, and insufferable family constantly
squabble among themselves, delight in ridiculing others, and refuse to admit their obvious ignorance and limitations. Their visit
to the opera is a masterful scene of satirical representation. From
the moment of their arrival, when they cannot locate the entrance,
to their derogatory comments after the last musical note, their attempt to carry off the evening grandly is an abysmal failure. Step
by step, Fanny exposes their stupidity. They are aghast at ticket
prices, astonished at the use of Italian, annoyed at the continuous
singing, amazed at the audience's fine dress, and amused at the
singer's unnatural poses. No previous eighteenth-century novel
captured the manners of gauche, ignorant, and uncultured people
in as incisive and amusing a fashion. Fanny's opera scene is a
masterpiece of its kind.

Much of this achievement is due to Fanny's being most at ease
in her characterization of Mr. Smith and the Branghtons because
of her ability to write realistic middle-class dialogue. Often she in-
jects slang or colloquialisms effectively. Mr. Branghton talks about
seeing some *"crinkum-crankum"* at the opera, Tom refers to his
stingy father as being "so bit," and his sisters constantly use "monstrous" as an intensive ("monstrous dear," "monstrous ugly"). Frequent "a'n't's" punctuate their conversation, along with "he
don't's." Particularly characteristic is their introductory use of the
exclamation "lord" and their reference to Evelina as "Miss."

"Lord, Polly, only think! Miss never saw her papa!"

"Lord, how odd!" cried the other; "why, then, Miss, I suppose
you wouldn't know him?" [17]

The Branghtons were so memorable, so vivid, so life-like that
Dr. Johnson and others often referred to them and quoted them.

The aristocratic characters—Lord Merton, Mr. Coverley, Mr.
Lovel, Mrs. Beaumont, and Lady Louisa Larpent—are unconvincing and unrealistic. Fanny may have had difficulty in depict-

ing these individuals because she was not so familiar with them as she was with middle-class people. Two of the characters, for example, come from the stage rather than from life. Lady Louisa Larpent is modeled after Sheridan's Lydia Languish, and Mr. Lovel is the traditional fop. The other characters are too arrogant and discourteous to be believable.

Fanny satirizes the fashionable characters by having them talk and act crudely, by having Evelina disparage their manners and morals, and by having Mrs. Selwyn ridicule them mercilessly. This acid-tongued woman (who may have been named because her victims could *seldom win* over her) is patterned after Richardson's Anna Howe or Charlotte Grandison, the lively ladies in *Clarissa* and *Sir Charles Grandison*. While Mrs. Selwyn constantly provides amusement at the expense of the aristocrats, and sometimes good-naturedly chides Evelina and Lord Orville, she is too aggressive, domineering, outspoken, and superior to serve as an exemplary character.

No doubt exists about Fanny's attitude towards this "modern" woman. The evidence is overwhelming: Mr. Villars is "disgusted at her unmerciful propensity to satire"; Evelina talks about the enemies that her "unbounded severity" creates, and refers unfavorably to her *"masculine"* understanding and manners; and Sir Clement objects to her incessant talking and to the "unbounded license of her tongue," which in *"a woman"* is intolerable. Although Fanny is a feminist in many respects, she disapproved of women talking, acting, or being like men, and shared the views of her feminine readers who realized that women were different and not equal.

Evelina's tremendous popularity in its day stemmed from its great appeal to middle-class ladies. It allowed them vicariously to mingle with fashionable people, attend popular places, and learn the social amenities. It furnished them with models to emulate (Lord Orville) and to avoid (the Branghtons). It enabled them to dream, to weep, and to laugh. Most of all, however, it provided them with a lifelike heroine who found happiness not because of her sexual attraction (Pamela), her death (Clarissa), or her courage (Sophia), but because of her virtue and conformity, two qualities within the reach of middle-class maidens.

Evelina is the eighteenth-century version of the girl next door who makes good in the high society of the big city. To thousands of women, she represented the Cinderella that they could become without a fairy godmother of a pumpkin coach. In an age when women could fulfill themselves only in marriage, and when without large dowries they were frustrated by the difficulty of finding attractive and well-to-do husbands, Evelina became a culture-heroine who accomplished what numerous others aspired to. She was a beacon of hope in the darkness of middle-class feminine life.

CHAPTER 3

A Young Author's Entrance into the World

THE success of *Evelina* provided Fanny with experiences as interesting, improbable, and amusing as those encountered by her heroine. The novel, a best seller of its day,[1] reached the hands of Fanny's friends without their realizing that she was its anonymous author. Her record of their comments and reactions to *Evelina* comprises one of the more delightful sections of the six-volume *Diary*[2] covering her life from the publication of the novel in 1778 to her death in 1840.

Fanny's initial apprehension about being discovered as the author of *Evelina* was quelled by rumors that it had been written by Christopher Anstey, author of the satirical *New Bath Guide*. Gaining confidence about her anonymity because no one associated her with the novel, and about its reception because everyone was praising it, the shy Fanny began to enjoy hearing *Evelina* discussed without suffering from the fear or embarrassment of being recognized as its author. She even had courage enough to read her novel aloud to Mr. Crisp although she skipped the introductory ode lest her voice quaver and reveal her, and she noted that she read poorly due to the irrepressible "invisible embarrassment."

Soon Fanny received Charlotte's letter from London with a glowing account of Dr. Burney's reaction to the novel. After reading about *Evelina* in the *Monthly Review*, he immediately sent for a copy, hinting that he was aware of its authorship. Charlotte recorded that his eyes teared as he read the introductory ode (Fanny herself cried while reading this account). Later, when he had finished *Evelina*, Susan wrote that he considered it the best novel that he knew "excepting Fielding's, and, in some respects, *better* than his!" Dr. Burney disliked "Mirvan's trick upon Lovel" but admired the characterization of Lord Orville and "blubbered" at the scene between Evelina and her father. He ended by stating that the novel was "in a new style too, so perfectly innocent and natural," that he was "excessively pleased with it," and that it was "wrought up in a most extraordinary manner." [3]

I *Vanity or Modesty?*

From this point in her *Diary* Fanny records in minute detail every plaudit accorded *Evelina* except for obvious "flummery." While reading endless pages of favorable comments from innumerable individuals, one is struck by the egotism of this woman's meticulously compiling all this material about herself. At the same time, one notes that in person, although listening attentively if not avidly to everything being said about *Evelina*, the demure Fanny acts pained, embarrassed, flustered, and disconcerted. The discrepancy between such modest actions and such unrestrained accounts of acclaim requires some consideration.

One might view Fanny's modesty as an affected, superficial pose adopted for others, while actually she was a vain woman, enjoying every compliment paid her. Since her letters and journals went to others, she consciously or subconsciously seems to be attempting to enhance herself in their eyes. Because such self-glorification is out of keeping with her self-effacing demeanor, she must have deluded others with her demure ways or misrepresented the manner in which she truly reacted. As to the latter charge, no doubt exists. Throughout the sixty-odd years covered in the *Diary*, Fanny consistently appears as a modest, shy, reticent person. In addition, the few words that her contemporaries have written about her validate this description. Finally, she could not have sent letters to members of her family and Mr. Crisp, pointing out how upset she was at the attention and compliments paid her, if these people did not realize that she would respond in this fashion. Their letters indicate that she reacted as they expected. Family members were sympathetic, not surprised; they consoled and comforted her.

Yet even if Fanny's representation of herself is faithful, one might still question whether her subconscious has not belied her conscious. Can a truly modest person compile at such length the adulation given her? In answering this question, one should remember that the twenty-five-year-old author was catapulted from complete obscurity to London prominence in a few months. Previously, within her own family, Fanny had been recognized as anything but exceptional. Others eclipsed her in various ways. Hetty was highly regarded for her musical ability; James for his naval accomplishments; Charles for his intellectuality; Charlotte for her beauty; and Susan for her charm. Fanny, the "Old Lady," who never attended school, and learned to read late in life, remained in the background, overshadowed by her talented brothers and sisters. To such a young woman, the huge success and high praise accorded her novel seemed improbable. The tone of Fanny's entries in the *Diary* is not one of vanity but of incredulity. She is not boasting but asking, "Can this be happening to me?"

In addition, as Thomas Macaulay points out, she was not writing for publication but for "the eyes of two or three persons who had loved her from infancy, who loved her in obscurity, and to whom fame gave the purest and most exquisite delight." [4] The closely knit Burneys derived pleasure and satisfaction from one another's accomplishments. Fanny's was not only a personal triumph but a family one. Recording the compliments paid her was a way of allowing other family members and "Daddy" Crisp to share in her happiness. He even prodded her to write more about what was said "of and to you."

Given a young woman with Fanny's family history, and the few readers of her diary, one can understand why she included so much material about herself. Although enjoying the praises and honors bestowed upon her, she maintained such a feeling of inferiority that she was terrified at meeting new people, particularly famous ones. She was always afraid that they would be disappointed in finding her to be a quiet, uninteresting young woman. Any time that she was stared at, pointed to, singled out, or paid particular attention, she became flustered, embarrassed, and disconcerted. If she could have remained anonymous, she would have enjoyed the adulation immensely. A proud father like Dr. Burney, however, could not be silent about his talented daughter.

One cannot blame him. Nearly everyone was reading *Evelina* and praising it. The *Monthly Review* heralded it as "one of the most sprightly, entertaining, and agreeable productions" of its kind.[5] Mrs. Cholmondeley, whose opinions were highly respected and widely quoted, recommended the novel to all her friends and acquaintances. Mrs. Thrale, the well-known mistress of Streatham, urged Mrs. Burney to read it because "there was a great deal of human life in it, and of the manners of the present time." She believed that it was written by someone who knew "the top and the bottom, the highest and the lowest of mankind." [6]

Among others lavish in their praises of *Evelina* were Edmund Burke, who sat up all night reading it, and Sir Joshua Reynolds, who called off all his obligations one day to finish it. The most thrilling compliment came from Dr. Johnson, who, upon completing the first volume, said that passages in it would "do honour to Richardson." Upon hearing his statement, Fanny could not contain herself: "Dr. Johnson's approbation!—it almost crazed me with agreeable surprise—it gave me such a flight of spirits, that I danced a jigg to Mr. Crisp." When the amazed Crisp later discovered the reason for her jubilation, he exclaimed in mock anger, "Why you little hussy,—you young devil! an't you ashamed to look me in the face, you *Evelina,* you! Why what a dance have you led me about it." [7]

II *Success at Streatham*

When Dr. Burney informed Mrs. Thrale that his daughter had written *Evelina,* she insisted that he bring her to Streatham. The young author's diffidence is most vividly revealed in her description of "the most consequential day" that she had spent since her birth.[8] She had "the fidgets" while approaching the magnificent home where Mrs. Thrale entertained people well known for their taste and learning. Fanny had heard about these distinguished gatherings from her father, who had attended many. She worried that the people at Streatham expected "a less awkward and backward sort of person that I was sure they would find."

Mrs. Thrale, however, was evidently forewarned about Fanny's timidity for she initially paid most of her attention to Dr. Burney, as if to assure Fanny that she did not regard her as "a show" and did not want to distress or frighten her. Even after they were together for some time, not even "a *hint*" was made about *Evelina.* Just before dinner Mrs. Thrale did inform Fanny that Dr. Johnson could repeat whole scenes from the novel by heart, and that Mr. Smith was his favorite character. Contrasted with Mrs. Thrale's tact and delicacy was "the attack" by a guest, Mr. Seward, who "astonished and provoked" Fanny by saying that she had "favoured the world" by writing *Evelina.* Typically, she does not repeat in the *Diary* the conversation with such flatterers.

When Dr. Johnson appeared at dinner, Fanny was moved to "delight and reverence" at the sight of him despite his "almost convulsive movements, either of his hands, lips, feet, or knees, and sometimes of all together." During dinner, he pleaded loss of appetite because he was "too proud now to eat. . . ." He explained that "sitting by Miss Burney makes me very proud today." After several other flattering statements to her, he spoke at length about his disappointment with Garrick's recent prologues and epilogues, and then about Sir John Hawkins, whom he characterized in the oft-quoted coinage as "a most unclubable man."

Evelina was never directly mentioned although once it was referred to when Dr. Johnson, talking about a lady's quarrel with a waiter for failing to serve her a full pint of ale, exclaimed, "Now Madame Duval could not have done a grosser thing!" Even Fanny enjoyed the laughter that went around the table, and recorded that she did not "glow, nor munch fast, nor look at my plate, nor loose [*sic*] any part of my usual composure!" She was grateful for Dr. Johnson's not naming her as the author of *Evelina,* and felt that such delicacy was "more flattering" than praise of the novel.

This was the first of many happy and stimulating visits to Streatham. Later Fanny resided there for weeks and months at a time. From the *Diary,* one wonders why Mrs. Thrale was attracted to her since Fanny seldom reveals herself to be an amusing, clever, or interesting conversationalist. Curiosity about her and admiration for her novel sustained her initial meetings with people, but the deepening friendships with Mrs. Thrale and Dr. Johnson, and with other leading figures later on in her life must have been established on more substantial grounds. Evidently Fanny did not reproduce her own bright quips and witticisms, or the scintillating observations that make much of her writing so refreshing. When she does present herself talking in some scenes, her role is minor and her statements merely sustain the conversation. Readers of the *Diary,* however, should realize that she must have been an interesting and fascinating person if she talked to any extent as she wrote, and if so many distinguished people enjoyed her friendship.

Originally Mrs. Thrale may have had an ulterior motive in being so kind. Her fame as a hostess rested for the most part upon her caging the literary lion, Dr. Johnson. Now she may have set her traps for the young lioness, Fanny Burney. But after several years of close friendship Mrs. Thrale loved and admired Fanny. She wrote that she had won her "Confidence & her Heart: 'tis the most valuable Conquest I ever *did* make, and dearly, very dearly, do I love my little *Tayo*. . . . I now respect her Caution and esteem her above all living Women." [9] When involved later in the agonizing problem of whether to marry Piozzi or not, Mrs. Thrale disregarded the advice of Fanny but still wrote that the novelist's "Skill in Life and Manners is superior to that of any Man or Woman in this Age or Nation." [10] This panegyric may have been caused by Mrs. Thrale's emotional state at the time; but, even allowing for excesses, the estimate is far greater than one would have conceived from reading about Fanny in the *Diary*.

Some of Mrs. Thrale's esteem and love stemmed from the contrasting personalities of the two women. She was a garrulous, sparkling, argumentative conversationalist; Fanny was an interested, receptive, avid listener. Mrs. Thrale's wit was sharp, biting, malicious; Fanny's nature was gentle, sweet, and innocent. Mrs. Thrale was vain, self-assertive, domineering; Fanny was modest, diffident, and meek. Yet their opposing personalities are inadequate to explain fully their intimate friendship. Each woman admired the other not only for traits that she herself lacked but also for the other's achievements, ability, and character. That Mrs. Thrale, who knew most of the talented women of the age, chose Fanny as her close friend is indicative of the young woman's charm and intelligence.

III *The Lovable Lexiphanes*

The first section of Fanny's *Diary* is most valuable for its portrait of the leading literary figure of the age, Dr. Samuel Johnson. Fanny evidently cast the same spell over him that she wove over such older men as Mr. Crisp, Richard Owen Cambridge, and Sir Joshua Reynolds. Johnson was never angry, curt, annoyed, or harsh to her. She stated that she would "always vouch for his kindness, as far as regards myself." But she did more than this: by failing to reveal his temper, his irascibility, his melancholy, and his irritability in her *Diary*, she subordinated this aspect of his personality. Only once, in describing an argument between him and Sir William Pepys, did she suggest the extent of Johnson's vehemence; but then she vitiated it by stressing how he bore Mrs.

Thrale's rebuke of his conduct with "patience and quietness." Moreover, Fanny continued by pointing out that "such a man's confessing himself wrong is almost more amiable than another man being steadily right." [11]

What she wrote about Johnson, however, is highly informative. Many of his unfavorable characteristics appear in Boswell's *Life;* the Johnson that Fanny described is seldom revealed in it. To her, he was gentle, flirtatious, admiring, affectionate, good-natured, sympathetic, tactful, comforting, and entertaining. There was something playful but kind in his teasing his "little Burney" about her bashfulness. It may have been Johnson's fondness for young people that made him so fatherly to Fanny. It may have been his charitable and protective instinct that responded to the plight of the shy, modest author on display at Streatham. It may have been his patron-like spirit which made him sympathetic to talented individuals, such as Goldsmith, who were ill at ease in society. Whatever the reason, Fanny saw little of Johnson's somber, melancholy, and pessimistic nature. Instead, she found him gay, whimsical, pleasant, and playful. What reader of Boswell could believe that "Dr. Johnson has more fun, and comical humour, and love of nonsense about him" than anyone else that Fanny ever saw? She wrote that she was frequently thrown into "tittering and ridiculous fits" at his antics.

Fanny's portrayal of Johnson supplements rather than negates the impression left by Boswell. The picture is not that of the great Lexiphanes pontificating to his male friends at the coffeehouse or club. In the *Diary* he is a relaxed, gracious, charming gentleman discussing life and literature in mixed company at dinner or in the parlor. His account of Bet Flint, Laurinda, Hortensia, and Mrs. Pinkethman—some ladies of the town with literary pretensions whom he had befriended—made Fanny "die with laughing." [12] He so frequently enjoyed poking fun at her that at one point she wrote that "he *wits* me eternally." [13] But his laughter was affectionate, not derisive; it was motivated by fondness, not ridicule.

Dr. Johnson's absorbing concern with women's clothes is another generally unknown aspect of his nature. Fanny observed that he always commented on the dress of the ladies, sometimes indicating his disapproval with such vehemence that invited guests returned home to change their cap or gown. His views on dress, like his ideas about many other matters, were based upon sound common sense. He objected to ladies blindly following the dictates of fashion. Even though every woman at court was wearing a bandeau, Mrs. Thrale should not. In his typical manner, he explained how unbecoming it would be to this four-foot-eleven-inch woman: "that which seems nothing upon a Patagonian, will become very conspicuous upon a Lilliputian, and of you there is so little in all, that one single absurdity would swallow up half of you." [14]

Most appealing of all Johnson's characteristics revealed in the *Diary* was his protectiveness towards Fanny. When her name once appeared in a crude satirical pamphlet, Fanny became so upset from this public ridicule that she could not eat, drink, or sleep for more than a week. Hearing about her reaction from Dr. Burney, Johnson visited Fanny. When he found others there, "he had the delicacy and goodness to forbear coming to the point." Yet he was able to comfort and console her without their realizing it. Fanny found him to be more understanding about her problem than anyone else. In her time of trouble, he was "more kind, more good-humoured, more flattering to me than ever." [15]

The *Diary* also reveals Dr. Johnson's friendship and affection for the Thrales in numerous vivid domestic scenes. Shortly after he met Fanny at Streatham, he told her that "these are as good people as you can be with; you can go to no better house; they are all good nature; nothing makes them angry." [16] Praises like this of his host and hostess serve as a corrective for Boswell's biased view of Mrs. Thrale. The relationship between Dr. Johnson and Mrs. Thrale lasted for nearly twenty years. Each admired, respected, understood, and was fond of the other; yet each was aware of the other's faults and frequently pointed them out. Fanny described not only their pleasant association with each other but also the final break and the bitterness ensuing from Mrs. Thrale's marriage to Piozzi.

IV *Romance Comes to Mrs. Thrale*

This sensational affair that shocked London society is almost completely excised from the *Diary*. During the several years that it was the common topic of conversation, people did not understand how Mrs. Thrale could consider marrying Piozzi, her daughter's former singing teacher. Not only was he socially beneath her, but he was poor, a foreigner, and a Catholic. Mrs.

Montagu literally believed that Mrs. Thrale was out of her mind,[17] a sentiment shared by others. No one realized that the forty-one-year-old woman had finally found the love and affection that she craved.

Married for convenience when young to a man twelve years older—the wealthy, brusque Henry Thrale—she bore him twelve children (of whom only four lived) and endured his blatant unfaithfulness. She also worked hard in nursing and caring for Dr. Johnson; and after her husband's death she struggled with the financial problems of his brewery to prevent its bankruptcy. For many months she was torn between her ardent desire for Piozzi, and the opposition of her daughter Queeney, of Fanny, and of other friends. Finally the promise of a new, carefree life with a kind, romantic man resembling her father proved too much to resist. At almost the last minute, she notified Dr. Johnson of her marital plans, unwilling to consult him earlier for fear of his reaction. He wrote a thunderous reply; she answered with dignity. To Dr. Johnson's credit, he then forwarded his blessing and good wishes for the marriage. Happiness Mrs. Thrale found, but she lost nearly all her friends, including Dr. Johnson and Fanny.[18]

This entire episode is mentioned only indirectly in the *Diary*. Once Fanny refers to "the very unhappy Mrs. Thrale"; upon another occasion she writes how much she pities her, but tells Susan that she has not discussed the subject with anyone and will not, despite the many rumors. In addition, one published Thrale letter ends, "Ah, Burney! you little know the suffering, and, I will add, the patient suffering of your H.L.T." [19] The absence of other information about the Thrale Piozzi affair is explained in a note added to the *Diary* later. Fanny wrote that she had destroyed many letters under the "golden rule" policy, and had left only those that would exonerate Mrs. Thrale from "the banal reproach of yielding unresisting to her passions." [20]

Fanny also failed to mention her numerous efforts to deter Mrs. Thrale, and her delicate role as mediator between Mrs. Thrale and Queeney.[21] She did not, however, expunge Dr. Johnson's reaction to the wedding. He told Fanny that he had burned all of Mrs. Thrale's letters and driven her from his mind. He added that he never spoke of her and wanted never to hear of her.

Fanny's attitude towards Mrs. Thrale was more tolerant. The young author had spent many hours discussing the problem with

her, listening to her agonize over the dilemma, and watching her
health suffer from the strain. Although disapproving of the marriage, Fanny reconciled herself to it. But her coolness to Piozzi,
reflected in her congratulatory letter to the couple, provoked Mrs.
Thrale and caused a rift that never healed. Despite this rebuff,
Fanny always felt grateful and loyal to her friend. Once, although
admitting that Mrs. Thrale's action was indefensible, Fanny
stated, "I should be the last to forget all that had made me love
her before it was committed." [22]

V   Death Comes to Dr. Johnson

The departure of Mrs. Thrale was soon followed by the death
of Dr. Johnson. In the fall of 1783, when Fanny visited him at
Bolt Court, he appeared to be in fine form. He talked to her with
"as much fire, spirit, wit, and truth of criticism and judgment" as
ever. As she was leaving, he called her back for a moment to ask
"in a solemn voice, and in a manner the most energetic. . . . 'Remember me in your prayers!'" [23] These were his last words to her;
for, although she visited his house frequently afterwards, he was
always too ill to see her. Dr. Burney reported once that Johnson
apologized for being unable to see Fanny, hoped that she was
praying for him, and in a light moment slyly stated, "I think that I
shall throw the ball at Fanny yet." [24] Nine days later, at the age of
seventy-five, Dr. Johnson died.

The thirty-three-year-old Fanny confined her grief to a brief
paragraph, paying tribute "to the ever-honoured, ever-lamented"
man, mentioning that Charles and her father attended the funeral, and stating that she had cried all day, and was doing so as
she wrote in her *Diary*. Then stoically she ended with the statement that she would "pass over what to mourn is now so vain." [25]
There is little evidence of sentimentality here or elsewhere in her
work.

VI   Other Notables

Because Fanny lived with the Thrales and Dr. Johnson for
much of the period 1778–1783, she wrote mainly about them. But
other well-known figures appear frequently in her pages. Most
captivating of all to Fanny was Edmund Burke, whom she praised
for being as charming as Garrick. She found it difficult to reproduce his conversation that darted so swiftly from subject to

subject. In addition, she warned her readers that what he said suffered in transcription because it was enhanced by his "clear, penetrating, sonorous, powerful" voice; his "noble" figure; his commanding air; his graceful address; and his eloquent language.[26]

Another important figure mentioned frequently during the Streatham years was Mrs. Elizabeth Montagu, the leading Blue Stocking. Although Fanny was often in her company, the *Diary* contains no examples of this brilliant woman's conversation. On two occasions Fanny compared her with Mrs. Thrale. The first time she noted that Mrs. Montagu "is always reasonable and sensible, and sometimes instructive and entertaining." Mrs. Thrale was the opposite: "always entertaining and instructive, and sometimes reasonable and sensible." [27] Later Fanny concluded that Mrs. Montagu "reasons well, and harangues well but wit she has none." Mrs. Thrale, on the other hand, had too much wit; "for when she is in spirits, it bursts forth in a torrent almost overwhelming." [28] Although these valuations are interesting, they do not compensate for a scene with the two ladies engaged in repartee. One wishes, for example, to have heard them in action the night at Bath when they "talked all the talk, and talked it so well, no one else had a wish beyond hearing them." [29]

Although other illustrious individuals are mentioned in this part of the *Diary*, none comes to life as do Mrs. Thrale and Dr. Johnson. Sir Joshua Reynolds, the great painter and member of Johnson's Club; Richard Brinsley Sheridan, the playwright and producer; and Arthur Murphy, the playwright, producer, and biographer, all appear in several scenes but relatively little effort was made to portray them. Others prominent in their day but somewhat obscure now are hardly represented at all. They include Christopher Ansley, author of the *New Bath Guide;* Mrs. Elizabeth Carter, translator of Epictetus and a famous Blue Stocking; Anthony Chamier, statesman and original member of Johnson's Club; Sir John Hawkins, biographer of Dr. Johnson; Mrs. Charlotte Lenox, author of the *Female Quixote;* and Dr. Joseph Warton, poet and editor of Pope.

VII *Problems of a Diarist*

This portion of the *Diary* is disappointing for these omissions. Yet when one recalls Fanny's purpose and audience, one can un-

derstand her lapses. She was concerned with her present readers
rather than future ones. What she set out to do was to write an
interesting, amusing account to members of her family and to a
few intimate friends. Because of Johnson's fame and fascination,
she tried to provide her readers with a lengthy and detailed description of him. This meant that she often ignored others. Once
she particularly regretted this limitation because Mrs. Thrale's
conversation was so entertaining, enlivening, intelligent, and
instructive that Fanny wished she could "record all she [Mrs.
Thrale] says, as all Dr. Johnson says." [30] But the physical act of
writing her journals and remembering what words were uttered
was taxing. Fanny made no notes at the time but jotted some
down later in her room or wrote from memory the following
morning, always striving for accuracy. Once she regretted being
unable to write more about Johnson because she "could not recol-
lect his exact words, and I do not choose to give him mine." [31]
That she reproduced Johnson's conversation faithfully is obvious
from a comparison with Boswell's *Life.* Both works testify to his
brilliant talk, which Fanny said was so much like his writing that
it was the same thing "to hear or to read him." [32]

The limitations imposed by her writing conditions benefited as
well as hindered her. *Evelina* and the *Early Diary* owe much to
their simple, natural, colloquial style. Fanny continued to write in
this manner in her *Diary,* feeling no need to impress her family
and friends with elegance or eloquence. But she was always concerned about making her readers see and hear what had occurred.
When the Corsican hero, General Paoli, told her about his experiences, she struggled to depict his pompous manner and to reproduce his broken English although she wrote that the effect might
not be as comical to read as it was in actuality. Once she refused
to repeat Murphy's many stories because "they won't do upon
paper." [33] This sense of immediate involvement at all times with
her audience is discernible throughout.

For this reason, her accounts of Sophy Streatfield's weeping
upon request, Mrs. Vesey's bizarre parties, Lady Miller's vase ceremony at Bath, and other social affairs are memorable. Instead
of resorting to summary, she presented events dramatically, sometimes giving only the dialogue, as if writing a play. Her only devi-
ation from verisimilitude was to assemble her characters first and

describe them individually before recording what they said. Naturally, the conversations were artistically selected and edited.

VIII *The Human Comedy*

Fanny's *Diary* abounds with odd, quaint, eccentric characters. Nowhere is this more apparent than in her descriptions at Streatham, Bath, and other homes and places where she mingled with the upper-middle and lower-upper classes during 1778–83. She particularly relished collecting colorful characters to amuse her readers. One favorite was Mr. Blakeney, an Irish gentleman, between sixty and seventy who attempted to pass for about forty. More than fifteen pages are devoted to this individual who was "gallant, complaisant, obsequious, and humble to the fair sex" but otherwise "swaggering, blustering, puffing, and domineering." In talking about going to a ball one evening, he informed Mrs. Thrale that "there was a time when—tol-de-rol, tol-de-rol (rising, and dancing, and singing), tol-de-rol!—I could dance with the best of them! but, now a man, forty and upwards . . . tol-de-rol! —there was a time!" [34]

Mr. Crisp had written Fanny earlier that her days at Streatham would be the happiest in her life because she would never find another set of people like those gathered there. Fanny realized it. She noted that "the world, and especially the Great World, is . . . filled with absurdity of various sorts, now bursting forth in impertinence, now in pomposity, now giggling in silliness, and now yawning in dulness. . . ." [35] She was tempted to write about it all in something besides letters; in fact, to do so was too tempting to resist.

CHAPTER 4

The Death of a Comedy and the Birth of a Novel

WHILE Fanny lived at Streatham, Mrs. Thrale was constantly after her to write a comedy. She not only recognized Fanny's particular talent but also her financial need. If Fanny could turn out a play, she could capitalize on the reputation of her novel. The thirty pounds that *Evelina* brought was a pittance compared with the nearly four hundred pounds received by Hannah More for a tragedy.[1] Dr. Johnson agreed with Mrs. Thrale. One day after laughing heartily to himself, he explained that he had a notion that Fanny would begin her career as a dramatist with a comedy about Streatham—"Yes! 'Streatham—a Farce!'"

Fanny was already at work; in May, 1779, *The Witlings* was completed.[2] Its plot is typical of romantic comedies: the young lovers, Cecilia and Beaufort, are kept from marrying by his aunt, Lady Smatter, when Cecilia loses her fortune through the carelessness of Stipend, a broker. At the play's end the lovers are joined when Mrs. Smatter decides to approve of their marriage rather than be publicly lampooned by Censor.

According to Mrs. Thrale, a successful comedy needed "a scene or two of the pathetic kind."[3] In *The Witlings* Fanny emotionally exploits Cecilia's economic plight. The impoverished girl not only loses Beaufort and cannot pay the rent, but subsequently prepares to serve as a menial companion to Mrs. Hollis and her children in a foreign country. Much crying, sighing, philosophizing, and lamenting accompany her mounting distresses. Rhapsodic lines like the following characterize her speeches: "Hast thou not, Fortune, exhausted, now, thy utmost severity?—reduced to Poverty,—abandoned by the World,—betrayed by Beaufort,—what more can I fear?"[4] Beaufort talks in kind; and, in the sentimental climactic scene, he kneels before Cecilia, begging forgiveness.

Such scenes and action probably satisfied Mrs. Thrale. What did not please her was the satirical subplot involving Lady Smatter and the members of the Esprit Society. This woman, who constantly misquotes her favorite authors—Swift, Pope, and Shakespeare—and is the head of a literary club, closely resembled Mrs. Montagu: both organized literary groups, admired Shakespeare, possessed enormous wealth, and served as their nephew's guardians. Fanny's satire also included other Blue Stockings, although in a more general way. Acts II and IV are devoted to the eccentricities of club members at their meetings. Among the people are Mrs. Sapient, who is more ignorant and superficial than Mrs. Smatter; Jack, who is always in a hurry although he has nothing to do; his father, Codger, who thinks but never acts, and talks but never says anything; Mrs. Voluble, who chatters on incessantly about trivia; and Dabbler, a poetaster patronized by Lady Smatter.

Most of the satire is achieved through the obvious folly and self-contradictions of the characters. Mrs. Sapient, for example, expounds at length about the unimportance of a person's attire, and then orders the milliner to take great care in trimming her hat. Some of the satire results from the comments of the monitor character, Censor, who catches Lady Smatter in misquotations, points out that the learned ladies never listen to each other, and exposes Dabbler's feigned extemporaneous poem. Censor also plays an important role in the plot by persuading Beaufort to stay with Lady Smatter, and by blackmailing her at the end into allowing the lovers to marry. In addition, he states the theme of the play: "Is not security from want the basis for all Happiness? And if you undermine that, do you not lose all possibility of enjoyment?" [5]

Fanny pinned her financial hopes on *The Witlings*. It contained all the eighteenth-century ingredients necessary for success: a sentimental love story; a host of eccentric "humour" characters; savage satire at the expense of the literary ladies; and rollicking farce, especially in the scene when Bob Voluble creates a horrendous mess trying to clean up his mother's parlor. It was exactly the play that the Streathamites knew that she could write, urged her to write, and hoped she would write.

I *The Sting of Satire*

But *The Witlings* was also more than anyone had anticipated or expected. It was one thing for Fanny to satirize the Branghtons or the fashionable people at Mrs. Beaumont's; it was another to ridicule the literary ladies. Dr. Johnson had once playfully suggested to Fanny that she attack Mrs. Montagu, but he meant it to be done in a parlor, not a public playhouse. When Dr. Burney read the first draft of the play with Mr. Crisp at Chessington, both men were shocked; both urged her to suppress it. Dr. Burney realized that his future as a music-master depended upon maintaining and acquiring friends and not creating enemies. "Daddy" Crisp argued partially on literary grounds, pointing out that *The Witlings* resembled Molière's *Les Femmes Savantes* but was not as good. Although Fanny claimed never to have read the play, their themes are similar, as are the presence of the salon ladies and the poetaster, and the developing of complications through the loss of the heroine's fortune. However, both Mr. Crisp and Dr. Burney mainly disapproved of *The Witlings* because they felt that it would damage Fanny's reputation.

A dejected Fanny accepted their advice, not only for her own sake but because she realized that the play might jeopardize her father's good name. Keenly disappointed at having to put aside her work, she also felt bitter about wasting her precious time, stolen with difficulty at odd moments here and there during the day and evening. Yet, rather than remain "sulky and dejected," she decided to produce something "less reprehensible" as soon as she could stop thinking about her "enfans." Finally she brought herself to bid them farewell: "Good night Mr. Dabbler!—good night Lady Smatter,—Mrs. Sapient,—Mrs. Voluble,—Mrs. Wheedle,—Censor,—Cecilia,—Beaufort,—and you, you great oaf, Bobby! —good night! good night!" [6]

But *The Witlings* was not easily forgotten. When Sheridan and Murphy each wanted to stage the play, practically guaranteeing its success, Fanny and Dr. Burney weakened. But Mr. Crisp remained adamant and carried the day. It was just as well because a performance of the play would have marred Fanny's personal life. The formidable Mrs. Montagu would have retaliated by lampooning and ridiculing Fanny in various ways. Such an experience would have been highly injurious to the sensitive young woman. Mrs. Thrale, realizing full well what would occur, approved of withdrawing the play: "Fanny Burney has pleased me today—She resolves to give up a Play likely to succeed; for fear it may bear hard upon some Respectable Characters." [7]

II *The Scars*

Suppressing the play was wise in view of Fanny's sensibilities but detrimental to her artistic development. The traumatic experience made her acutely aware that her reputation depended not only on her readers' response to her literary work but also on their impression of her and her relationships with others. Consequently, Fanny's work became taut and self-conscious for many years to come reflecting her constant concern with her image. This obsession restricted and inhibited her.

Moreover, her distressing experience with *The Witlings* made her realize that it was safer not to write about her own experience. *Evelina* was a projection of herself. *The Witlings* was drawn from her observations of the fashionable world at Bath and Streatham with the Thrales. In future years she took pains to divorce her work from her own life. Unfortunately, the less her novels dealt with what she knew best, the poorer they became.

Just as Fanny became overly self-conscious and restrained, and depended more upon literary tradition than life for her material, so she turned away from satire. The stinging rapier of *The Witlings* was dangerous; it could draw blood. It was much safer, for instance, to follow Mr. Crisp's advice about writing spirited, useful, moral comedies about family follies. But Fanny's bent was satirical. Although she could not eliminate this spirit completely from her writing, she managed to curb it. Inasmuch as she did so, her work suffered; and literature is the poorer today. What she did to the Branghtons might have been done not only to the Blue Stockings but to court members, music patrons, and French aristocrats. The demise of *The Witlings* ended all such efforts.

III *The Need to Write*

Now that the play was put aside, Dr. Burney and Mr. Crisp clamored more than ever about the importance of getting something in print before *Evelina* was forgotten. Neither man had to mention financial matters to Fanny; although unconcerned about luxuries or anything above material needs, she was aware of the family's limited resources. Dr. Burney's income was high, but his expenses were huge from traveling abroad to gather material for his books and from maintaining a proper appearance among the fashionable people with whom he worked.[8] Under such circum-

stances, he was unable to save much or to set anything aside for
the girls' dowries. Even though fine gentlemen proposed to "portionless" heroines in *Evelina* and *The Witlings,* Fanny knew that
this practice occurred rarely in life. Her own experience with Mr.
Crutchley at this particular time was a case in point.

Jeremiah Crutchley, a frequent visitor at the Thrale's (and ru-
mored to be Thrale's illegitimate son),[9] resided at Streatham
while working as executor of his estate. Fanny's romantic interest
in him is first apparent in the aftermath to some playful matchmaking by Mrs. Thrale. Crutchley replied indignantly to a remark
linking him with Fanny. Although Fanny had also objected, she
felt offended at his reaction: "Was it not highly insolent?—and
from a man who has . . . given me a thousand reasons . . . to
think myself very high indeed in his good opinion and graces?"
What really rankled her followed: "But these rich men think
themselves the constant prey of all portionless girls, and are always upon their guard, and suspicious of some design to take
them in." [10]

In time this wound from Crutchley healed, especially because
he obsequiously courted her and begged to be taken back into her
good graces. Afterwards, during the spring of 1782, most of her
journal-letters described conversations with him. The two of them
teased each other, quarreled slightly, discussed morality, and otherwise enjoyed each other's company. Mr. Crutchley was unattractive and unconventional; but he was wealthy, honorable, and
intelligent. Fanny certainly admired and respected him; according to Mrs. Thrale, she loved him.[11] That she was deeply disappointed in his failure to propose is certain.

The relationship between Fanny and Crutchley is analogous to
that between the hero and the heroine of the novel that Fanny
was writing at the time. Each woman was distressed at receiving
the flattering attentions of an admirer for a long time without any
declaration of his intentions. In *Cecilia,* Mortimer Delvile finally
announced his love; in life, Jeremiah Crutchley never did.

The experience with Crutchley may have renewed Fanny's interest in the economic plight of middle-class women. All her heroines after *Evelina* are involved with financial problems, either
worrying about the loss of money, ways to acquire it, or the means
of repaying debts. In all instances, money is a key factor in their
relationships with men. More than any other eighteenth-century

heroines after Fielding's *Amelia*, Fanny's women are constantly concerned with financial problems.

Well aware of the money to be realized from another novel, Fanny began one. *Evelina* had been a labor of love; *Cecilia* was a tortuous, tiresome burden, causing Fanny many hours of anguish and ill health. Family problems during its writing were distracting. Dr. Burney's initial objection to Susan's marrying Captain Molesworth Phillips, a hero of Cook's expedition, precipitated a minor crisis. The family was also upset when Charles was rejected for ordination. Then Esther became quite ill.

Despite all obstacles Fanny persisted. She circulated the first volume to her father and friends, rather than waiting until she completed the work as she had done with *The Witlings*. Favorable reactions poured in. Her father thought that it was superior in design and execution to *Evelina*. Mrs. Thrale agreed, stating that *Evelina* was "a baby" to it. Mr. Crisp was enthusiastic, saying that it was better than anything that had appeared since Fielding and Smollett. Their excitement about *Cecilia* spread rapidly. People everywhere bothered Fanny about it despite her desire to keep it "snug till the last." She complained also about the hurry to have it appear in print. Merely copying the five volumes without revising and correcting them required about ten weeks. Yet Dr. Burney, who had sold the copyright for two hundred fifty pounds, promised the publishers, Payne and Cadell, that it would be ready in a month. Although *Cecilia* went to the press without Fanny's being able to revise carefully as she had intended, her few changes indicate an awareness of the novel's prolixity and circumlocutions. How much better *Cecilia* would have been if she had had additional time must remain a conjecture.

CHAPTER 5

A Novel of Love, Pride, and Money

I N *Cecilia* Fanny strove to duplicate the success of *Evelina*. To
do so, she packed her elaborate novel with two main plots,
several subplots, numerous characters from various social strata,
and such sensational events as a duel, a secret marriage, a case of
temporary insanity, an apoplectic stroke, and a suicide. The result
was a far cry from the peaceful little social world revolving slowly
before Fanny's satirical eye in *Evelina*. Not only does *Cecilia*
have too much of all things but too much of the wrong things. At
Streatham people praised Fanny for the amusing scenes depicting
the Branghtons and Mr. Smith, not for the sentimental ones involving Macartney or Sir John Belmont. *Cecilia* contains some
comic touches but few sustained satirical effects. Instead, the
novel moves like a soap opera from one emotional crisis to another. Fanny's failure to realize the nature and extent of her genius results in a disappointing although interesting work.

I *Love and Money*

Cecilia is primarily concerned with financial and marital problems. Each is treated in a separate half of the novel, being linked
only tenuously. Like *Evelina*, the story begins with the departure
of a young country girl, Cecilia, for London. Having recently lost
her father and uncle, she stays with one of her three guardians,
Mr. Harrel, whose profligacy and inhumanity soon become apparent. Cecilia is torn between helping him out of his financial difficulties, brought on by extravagance and gaming, or allowing him
to suffer the humiliating consequences. Fearing his threats to kill
himself, believing his assurances, and hoping for his reformation,
Cecilia eventually loans him nearly all of her money. This sum
proves to be insufficient. Consequently, in a theatrical episode at
Vauxhall, Harrel, surrounded by a grotesque group comprised of
his wife, friends, and creditors, drinks champagne, sings gaily,

and then commits suicide. With this macabre scene, the first half of the novel virtually ends.

The second part of *Cecilia* deals with the harrowing love affair and the ensuing complicated marital efforts of the heroine and Mortimer Delvile, son of another guardian. Their main problem stems from a farfetched plot device: a clause in her deceased uncle's will stipulates that Cecilia's husband must adopt her surname (i.e., become Mr. Beverley) or she will lose her inheritance. Compounding this difficulty is the abnormal aristocratic obsession of the Delviles, who retain a distinguished family name and a rundown castle, but have no money. At the novel's end, after Cecilia and Mortimer have completed love's obstacle course, one containing every conceivable misunderstanding and misinterpretation, and resolved numerous dilemmas between love and duty, they agree on what should have been obvious from the beginning—to marry and forego the money from Cecilia's uncle.

This sketchy plot summary does not suggest the numerous subplots, the range of characters, or the treatment of various thematic ideas. In addition to the financial problems of the Harrels in the first half and to the marital difficulties of the hero and heroine in the second half, Fanny employs the Belfield family to create additional complications. The son, referred to as Mr. Belfield, and the daughter Henrietta possess integrity, sensitivity, and delicacy despite their lower-middle-class origin; the widowed Mrs. Belfield, however, is as vulgar as the Branghtons. The struggle of the young people to social position parallels Cecilia's efforts to be socially approved by the Delviles as Mortimer's wife. Henrietta Belfield—a simple, sweet Evelina—illustrates the plight of a lower-middle-class woman with all the qualities necessary to attract a fine gentleman—beauty, virtue, delicacy, modesty—except money and refinement. Although brokenhearted by Mortimer's love for Cecilia, Henrietta recovers and eventually marries Arnott, an innocuous but wealthy, kind country gentleman.

Her brother's story is far more complex. Like Henrietta, he also complicates the love story. Just as Mortimer suspects Cecilia of loving Belfield by misunderstanding her benevolent interest in him, so Cecilia misunderstands Mortimer's similar interest in Henrietta. But Belfield plays a larger role. Educated at great sacrifice to his family, he has associated with the sons of aristocrats. Having acquired their tastes and habits, he now finds it difficult to

accept his social station and to work for a living. In search of the
good life, he becomes a romantic nonconformist, moving from position to position, including one as a common laborer and another
as an idealistic writer.

After all occupations prove disillusioning, Belfield finally accepts a commission in the army. Even though Fanny indicates her
disapproval of his tendencies towards individualism and nonconformity, she treats him sympathetically rather than satirically.
The hero and heroine are kind and considerate towards Belfield,
believing that he is worth helping despite his lack of "steadiness
and prudence." Fanny also points out that he is "full of genius,"
but too "imaginative, wild, and eccentric." Such an individual
cannot find happiness outside of society or within it unless he is
wealthy.

II   *Of People and Their Personalities*

One might deplore the plethora of plot material if the characters were rendered well. What contributes to Fanny's success in
Evelina is that the simple plot allowed her to concentrate on
developing her heroine and others. In *Cecilia* the complex plot
overshadows the characters. Moreover, there is little comparison
between the natural girlish charm of Evelina and the antiseptic
personality of the poised, mature Cecilia. Although the latter learns
something about the social conventions of fashionable London
life, she does so without the humiliation and embarrassment that
made Evelina into a three-dimensional character. Cecilia's social
faux pas and her indiscretions, except for her imprudence in loan-
ing Harrel money, are insignificant. Depicted as high-principled,
beautiful, and intelligent, Cecilia remains a paragon throughout
with neither the depth nor complexity to be lifelike.

As for the other characters with important roles, not one is well-
motivated, plausible, or convincing. Monckton, Cecilia's diabolical mentor, is hardly credible with his ceaseless malevolent schem-
ing to keep her single until his wife dies. Lord Delvile (his name is
a play upon "devil") has no other dimension than that of the self-
important haughty aristocrat bent upon preserving at all cost his
family heritage. Nowhere does he display any concern or sympathy for his son or wife. Lady Delvile, whom Cecilia comes to
admire and respect, is sketched in greater detail; but she never
reveals any of the frustrations she supposedly suffers from living

with a husband that she was forced to marry. The Harrels are also flat characters, being obsessed with luxury and extravagance. Neither their financial reverses nor Cecilia's pleadings dissuade them or cause them to engage in soul-searching or to reveal any qualms about their way of life.

Mortimer Delvile, on the other hand, is torn throughout the second half of the novel between filial obedience and love for Cecilia. Despite this complexity, he is as wooden in his speech and actions as Lord Orville and other Grandison-like heroes. Mortimer was attractive to Cecilia, but to readers he is humorless and spineless, in addition to being stiff, bland, and boring.

Just as Fanny failed with her major characters, so she did with most of her minor ones. With only a few exceptions, their dominant traits are carried to such extremes that they become caricatures. On the upper social level are the foppish Meadows, who affects boredom; the garrulous social butterfly, Miss Larolles, who delights in clothes, auctions, and masquerades; the taciturn, insipid Miss Leeson, who can converse only with her supercilious friends; the affected Captain Aresby, who decorates his talk with French words and phrases; and Mr. Morrice, the sycophant lawyer, who changes his views to please his company. On the middle social level are Briggs, the repulsive miser; and the officious Hobson and obsequious Simpkin, both tradesmen, whose affected gentility cannot hide their coarse lust for money.

The weakness of all these comic figures is that they lose their fascination through overuse. Some are depicted well in early scenes. Particularly delightful are Miss Larolles' account of obtaining a ticket, dress, and hairdo at the last minute for the grand masquerade at Lord Darien's, Miss Leeson's inability to discuss any subject with Cecilia, and Mr. Briggs' strictures on economy and "sharpers." Fanny introduces these and other "humour" characters so repeatedly that the freshness and surprise so necessary for comic effect quickly vanish, and the exaggerated eccentrics soon lose their appeal.

Fanny is successful with some characters. Most amusing of these is Lady Honoria, the gay, impertinent "rattle," who plays practical jokes, chides Cecilia for blushing at the mention of Mortimer's name, and generally brightens up the many tedious sections of the novel with her wit and light banter. She is conceived in the tradition of Fanny's lively women who sacrifice grace, dignity, and decorum to levity, informality, and nonconformity. Unlike *Evelina's* Mrs. Selwyn, Honoria lacks the intelligence to be a satirist; however, her uninhibited remarks and her sprightly quips provide a much-needed relief from the sentimentality and high seriousness of the novel's second half.

Although Mrs. Belfield, the matchmaking mother, is a stock character, she differs from predecessors in her vulgarity and in her attempt to persuade a woman (Cecilia) to marry her son. Fanny is at her best in delineating the coarseness and boorishness of such individuals. Of all the characters, Mrs. Belfield is the most striking, although she is sometimes so obnoxious and overbearing that one has the impression that she is overdrawn.

Less plausible than Mrs. Belfield but equally interesting are Gosport and Albany. The former, Fanny's commentator, explains satirically and perceptively the ways of society to Cecilia. Just as Fanny had been careful to elucidate to readers of *Evelina* the dance conventions and other social codes, so she has her "country ladies" in mind again. To them, as well as to present readers, Gosport provides a delightfully entertaining commentary.

Albany, on the other hand, is a mysterious, melodramatic figure who haunts Cecilia with Cassandra-like wails of impending danger ("poor simple victim"), condemnations of fashionable people ("Oh mignons [*sic*] of idleness and luxury"), and requests ("give comfort to the fallen and dejected"). As a benevolent misanthrope, conceived in the tradition of Smollett's Mathew Bramble, Albany rants wildly in imabic pentameter, preaches a rigid and stern morality, and promulgates philanthropy as the only way of life leading to redemption and happiness. His appeal as a character lies in his uniqueness; although heightened beyond belief, he gains in the vivid dramatization of his character what he loses in verisimilitude. Well-motivated by a sentimentally tragic love experience, he functions at times like a Greek chorus with his misanthropic comments upon society; but he also serves on the plot level to rescue Cecilia from despondency and death at the end of the novel. Albany was the favorite character of Dr. Johnson and Dr. Burney.[1]

Edmund Burke, in a letter praising and thanking Fanny for writing *Cecilia*, mentions her "incredible variety of characters" and discreetly hints that perhaps "they are too numerous." [2] He rightfully objects to the multitude of minor figures cluttering the novel. It is as if Fanny reached into the notes that she wrote throughout most of her life about eccentric characters, pulled out a few choice specimens, and sprinkled them throughout the book.[3] With so many minor figures, exaggerated and overused, and with such poorly rendered major ones, *Cecilia* is not a first-rate novel.

III   *Cracks in the Craftsmanship*

Another weakness may be attributed to Fanny's faulty craftsmanship. *Evelina*'s epistolary form allows Fanny to relate events mainly in the natural, fresh, lively style of the seventeen-year-old heroine. Readers delight in the vivid dramatic scenes, and also enjoy the transitional passages in which Evelina comments on past events and discusses future ones. In *Cecilia,* however, Fanny assumes the role of omniscient author. The voice that she uses is not that of the ebullient young girl but of the elegant, polished, cultivated author who wrote the preface to *Evelina* and the letters of Mr. Villars with their balanced sentences, antitheses, circumlocutions, and inversions. The sparkling natural prose of her diaries and first novel is replaced, therefore, by a stilted, learned style that Fanny felt would impress others. The result satisfied her contemporaries but makes her novel less readable and enjoyable today.

The omniscient viewpoint also proves too much of a temptation to Fanny. *Evelina* forced her to confine herself mainly to the eyes and mind of a young girl. Because the angle of narration of *Cecilia* places no restraints upon her, she describes and discusses her characters instead of presenting them dramatically. As Cecil points out in writing about Mrs. Delvile, readers understand her but do not "see" her.[4] Lengthy analytic passages precede the introduction of most figures, thereby depriving the reader of the delight of self-discovery. These expository sections also detract from the vividness of the characters.

Given the opportunity to describe her characters directly to the reader, Fanny relies less on dialogue than she had in *Evelina*. Moreover, most of the recorded conversations consist of discussions between Cecilia and the Delviles, or among the Delviles themselves. All orate like characters in heroic tragedies and do not sound like living human beings. Except for Honoria, Fanny was as unable to reproduce the natural conversation of the upper

classes in her second novel as she had been in her first. The middle-
class characters—Briggs, Hobson, Simkin, and Mrs. Belfield—
speak almost as naturally as Mr. Smith and the Branghtons. Unhappily, in *Cecilia* the aristocrats do most of the talking; their
affected, inflated speeches are lifeless declamations that are
deadly to read.

As the omniscient author, Fanny also could moralize whenever
she felt like it; and she felt like it frequently. Once again, she was
catering to the taste of the day. Mrs. Delany, for example, stated
that no other book was so useful as *Cecilia*.[5] Because a novel is no
longer valued as a textbook on social conduct, Fanny's constant
moralizing is obtrusive and tedious.

Another weakness in craftsmanship stems from Fanny's inconsistent use of her role as omniscient author. Throughout the novel
she freely enters the minds of characters to disclose their thoughts.
Having selected this approach, one expects her to sustain it. Yet
she fails to do so with Albany, and she only partially does so with
Monckton. The latter's numerous schemes to thwart Cecilia from
falling in love and marrying are all revealed except for one: his
sending Miss Bennet to halt the secret wedding. In withholding
this vital fact Fanny gains suspense but does so unnaturally and
inconsistently. She is guilty of the same practice in failing to provide any information about the mysterious Albany although she
discusses all other characters openly and in detail.

The overuse of chance and coincidence is another fault in *Cecilia.* Fanny constantly brings characters together without regard
for probability. With thousands of people in London needing aid,
Albany escorts Cecilia to two women—Belfield's sister and
mother! Later Cecilia helps another unfortunate person who turns
out to be the "Pew-Opener," the only individual besides Monckton able to identify Miss Bennet. In addition to these and similar
improbable occurrences, both Mortimer and his father constantly
appear at exactly the most inopportune moments for Cecilia,
thereby continually misinterpreting her conduct and further complicating the action. Fortuitous circumstances not only keep the
lovers apart at first but bring them together at the end. Once a
thunderstorm provides the privacy and emotional atmosphere
conducive for mutual confessions. Later, after one of their endless
misunderstandings, Mortimer conveniently strolls within earshot
as Cecilia unburdens her soul to Fidel, his dog! These and similar

incidents do little more than slow down or speed up the action. Of more significance in resolving the conflict, and therefore of greater artistic weakness, are the stroke of Mrs. Delvile, the deaths of Mrs. Charlton and Lady Monckton, and the near death of Monckton.

IV Sense and Sentimentality

With little opportunity to revise *Cecilia*, Fanny left a poorly paced work that drags on and on until the reader is driven almost as mad as the heroine. This effect results mainly from the excess of sentimentality and from the lack of comic relief in the second half. The first part of *Cecilia* is practically devoid of pathos. Harrel's suicide is not emotionally exploited. His wife, unlike her eighteenth-century counterparts,[6] shares her husband's taste for luxury and extravagance, thereby negating any claim to pity or sympathy. The only concession to sentimentality is the story of Mrs. Hill and her five children.

In the second half, however, feminine readers had little opportunity to put down their handkerchiefs. Only Honoria's practical jokes, witticisms, and merriment break the high seriousness of endless passionate debates between Mortimer and Cecilia, Mortimer and his parents, and Cecilia and Lady Delvile. These deliberations temporarily culminate in a heartrending scene during which Cecilia's tears sway Mortimer to her side until his mother, shrieking that her brain is on fire, collapses from a broken blood vessel.[7] Near the novel's close, Cecilia trumps this action by going out of her mind after being subjected to several traumatic experiences. Seemingly on her deathbed, after Albany eulogizes her and prays with the assembled children, whom she previously helped, Cecilia recovers.[8]

The somber mood does not change at the end where the traditional saccharine finale is replaced by a bittersweet one. The hero and heroine have fortuitously inherited sufficient land and wealth to live moderately ever after, but all is not perfect. Cecilia states that she is left with the affections of Mortimer and Lady Delvile, "all the happiness human life seems capable of receiving:—yet human it was and as such imperfect!" What still troubles her is "her loss of fortune . . . to be thus portionless, tho' an HEIRESS." She rationalizes by finding that everyone has some misery. Hence "she checked the rising sigh of repining morality, and grateful with general felicity, bore partial evil with chearfullest resignation." [9]

This philosophical note epitomizes Fanny's concern with ideas throughout *Cecilia*. At one point she attempts to unify the novel by attributing all the difficulties to pride and prejudice.[10] But prudence and benevolence are concepts more germane to the action. The heroine's problems stem mainly from her irresponsible handling of money. Excluding *Moll Flanders*, no previous novel paid such attention to a character's wealth. Cecilia's fortune is regularly appraised, her expenditures are carefully itemized, and her balance is frequently calculated. Money, or specifically its loss, serves to link the novel's two sections by complicating her marital plans and by contributing to her breakdown. Money also plays a key role in shaping the destinies of others: lack of it creates Belfield's problems and limits Henrietta's social acceptance; extravagance with it ruins Harrel; greed for it obsesses Briggs; concern for it vulgarizes Hobson and Simkin; and need for it almost victimizes Mrs. Hill. Prudence about money is a dominant thematic idea in *Cecilia*.

Closely associated with this concept are the author's views about benevolence. Fanny generally adheres to the sentimental tradition of revealing the innate goodness of characters by their philanthropy. Harrel's disregard for the impoverished Hills makes him as detestable as Cecilia's concern for them makes her admirable. Mortimer's character is established by his generosity to Belfield and by other kind acts, such as helping the gypsy family. Albany, of course, is the personification of benevolence, and therefore is immediately befriended and trusted by Cecilia. Benevolence, however, must be curbed by prudence, as Fanny indicates when Cecilia is evicted as a result of being overly generous to the domestics and others.

What weakens the cogency of these thematic ideas and the effectiveness of the novel is Fanny's failure to solve the multifarious problems of the elaborate plot. Burdened by the complex structure of the novel, she was unable to focus on the obligations and limitations of the omniscient viewpoint, to restrict the didacticism and sentimentality, to achieve her former natural style, and to avoid relying heavily on chance and coincidence.

V *Pro and Con*

Despite its flaws, *Cecilia* is more interesting and moving than this analysis suggests. Several scenes of manners in the first half of the novel—the masquerade, the opera rehearsal, and the opera itself—are all presented in the lively, satirical style of *Evelina*. The climactic suicide episode, although tending to be theatrical, is skillfully done, partially due to the presence of Hobson and Simkin. Even the sentimental and melodramatic quality of the second half of *Cecilia* fails to obstruct completely its suspense, power, and vitality because of Fanny's ingenious ability to devise new and different situations. Although most of the comic characters are delineated with little subtlety, and many are no more than caricatures, as a group they are often vivacious and vivid. Some—Honoria, Mrs. Belfield, and Albany—are deftly depicted.

Unfortunately, Fanny attempted too much in *Cecilia*. She moved out of her element when she substituted sentiment for satire, the serious for the comic, the omniscient for the epistolary form, fashionable characters for middle-class ones, and a vast canvas for a small one. More detrimental perhaps than anything was her changed tone. *Evelina* was written by a gay, happy, charming person, amused at but tolerant of people and their shortcomings. The author of *Cecilia* finds little good in people and little happiness in life. Dr. Johnson could convincingly present this view in *Rasselas;* Fanny Burney lacked the wisdom, experience, and profundity to give credence to the same concept in *Cecilia*.[11] One even wonders whether she accepted it herself.

CHAPTER 6

A Lady Enters Court Life

THE popularity of *Cecilia* made Fanny more of a celebrity. Because the continual round of visiting and meeting people bored and fatigued her, she curtailed her social activities to three days a week. Not only the number but the nature of the affairs nettled her. Fanny describes vividly the adulation that she was subjected to at Mrs. Ord's, where everyone stood up, "contrary to all present customs in large meetings. . . ."[1] After being introduced, Fanny sat down, only to be praised in turn by each member of the gathering. Soame Jennys, the essayist, delivered "an eulogy unrivalled . . . for extravagance of praise." By this time Fanny felt like running away.

Yet all was not this unpleasant. Her visits frequently brought her into the company of George Cambridge, a charming, attractive young clergyman. Their romance, if such it can be termed, lasted for about eight years. The entire affair has been skillfully summarized by Hemlow and can be read in the unpublished letters and in the suppressed portions of the *Diary* in the Berg Collection.[2] This material discloses how much Fanny cared for George Cambridge and how her feelings were hurt as he courted her in public but failed to declare his affection in private. His continued silence about their relationship disturbed, distressed, and disappointed her. Yet she recorded every meeting, every glance, every kind word, and every hint of his affection. She knew that her age (she was three years older) and her lack of a dowry made her an unattractive choice for a clergyman. Yet she hoped. Susan and friends advised her to avoid seeing him. Circumstances finally forced her to do so.

A person who made life less painful for Fanny during these years of her unrequited love affair was Mrs. Delany. This venerable eighty-three-year-old lady, formerly a close friend of Swift, the Wesleys, and Handel, was highly respected and admired.

74

Fanny recorded the details of her first visit to Mrs. Delany's house
for dinner just as she had previously written at length about her
Streatham dinner with Dr. Johnson. Mrs. Delany reminded Fanny
of her beloved maternal grandmother, but she was also attracted
to the older woman by her charm, social eminence, and worldly
wisdom. The friendship with Mrs. Delany ripened and grew, particularly after she moved near Windsor Castle to a house provided, along with a pension, by King George III and Queen Charlotte, who visited her frequently.

Mrs. Delany informed Fanny that the King and Queen inquired
about her frequently, talked about her novels, and indicated their
interest in meeting her. To prepare Fanny for such an encounter,
Mrs. Delany briefed her on how to comport herself, emphasizing
that Fanny should not respond to the Queen in monosyllables.
Two days later, while playing Christmas games with a child,
Fanny glanced up to find a large man with a star standing before
the only door in the room. Petrified, she could not sneak away.
The scene that followed with the King, and with the Queen, who
entered later, is the subject of a twenty-one page account that is
particularly memorable because Fanny writes of her awkwardness and shyness with more humor and introspection than she
usually displayed.[3] The added perspective gained by her good-
naturedly calling attention to her shortcomings enlivens the report. To the King's inquiry, for example, about why she wrote
Evelina, she finally stammered, "I thought—sir—it would look
very well in print!" Fanny confessed that this was the "silliest
speech" that she had every made. Later, after the Queen arrived,
Fanny realized that she was replying to Her Majesty's questions in
monosyllables. "Oh shocking! shocking!" she wrote in mock
horror.

Many meetings between Fanny and the royal family followed.
When a vacancy occurred in their household, they offered the position to Fanny, believing that she would eagerly accept it. She
did, but only after she had exhausted every other possibility, including a letter to George Cambridge's sister explaining her situation and hinting that she could yet be saved from "a lasting
bond." Whether or not Miss Cambridge informed her brother is
not known; however, he did not act. Nor did anyone else.

Fanny had been selected in preference to "thousands of offered
candidates, of high birth and rank, but small fortune, who were

waiting and supplicating for places. . . ." [4] She was to have an
apartment, a footman, a maid, a coach to share with another, and
two hundred pounds a year. In return, as Second Keeper of the
Robes, Fanny was to assist the Queen with her dress and toilette.
To Dr. Burney, nearing sixty and often in poor health, the position meant honor to his family; the possibility of preferment to its
members through Fanny's influence; security to her; and to him,
relief from any financial concern about his unmarried, thirty-four-
year-old daughter. To Fanny, the position meant loss of freedom,
absence from her friends, and confinement for life.

Dr. Burney urged her to accept. There was no alternative. The
Diary poignantly describes the day when Dr. Burney and Mrs.
Ord brought Fanny to Windsor Castle.[5] Her apprehension and
sorrow are contrasted vividly with their happiness and satisfaction. Until walking the last fifty yards to the Queen's Lodge,
Fanny was able to hide her feelings. Then, on "the point of enter-
ing—probably for ever an entire new way of life," of giving up all
enjoyments, and of shattering "every dear expectation of life," she
cried so much that she alarmed her father. Before the Queen,
however, she was composed; and she was able to say to her father
later that evening, that Her Majesty's graciousness and kindness
convinced her that she would no longer be unhappy or have any
regret.

The unperceptive and unsuspicious Dr. Burney, anxious for any
assurance from his daughter, eagerly accepted her words at face
value. Fanny revealed her feelings and stoical attitude in a letter
to Susan: "I am married, my dearest Susan. . . . I was averse to
forming the union, and I endeavored to escape it; but my friends
interfered—they prevailed—and the knot is tied. What then remains but to make the best wife in my power?"

I Life at Court

Comprising about eleven hundred pages, the five-year account
of Fanny's court experiences is one of the more interesting sections of her *Diary*. Like Evelina or Cecilia, Fanny entered a
strange life and world; learned about the manners and morals of
its inhabitants; became involved in a lengthy, poignant love affair;
and struggled against the machinations of a cruel individual. Even
the modified happy ending and the host of comic characters are
reminiscent of a Burney novel.

Fanny's initial days at court were spent getting accustomed to the tedious routine of waking at six to prepare for the Queen's summons and then waiting to help her at midnight when she retired. During the interim Fanny's free time was occupied by the demands of dress and appearance (her hair had to be curled and craped twice a week), and by frequent social obligations with the King's equerries and Mrs. Schwellenberg, her superior. The demands upon her were as difficult to accept as her treatment. In person the Queen was always polite, gracious, and considerate. However, Fanny resented the ignominy of being summoned by a bell and being dismissed by the words, "Now I will let you go." Later Fanny realized that being told to leave in this fashion was an honor accorded only to people of the first rank, including the princesses; others left immediately upon completing their business, without being addressed.

Occasionally, adherence to protocol resulted in amusing episodes. The royal majesties were fortunately aware of Fanny's nearsightedness. Once it excused her failure to stand when the Queen entered the room; and upon another occasion, it condoned her walking past the King and his equerries, instead of halting and standing aside. The most diverting account of problems involving protocol is a report of an incident during the royal visit to Oxford.[6] Fanny's comic talents enable her to describe delightfully the ludicrous spectacle of the professors kissing the King's hand in various awkward ways, and then tottering, stumbling, and falling, as they backed away.

Despite these lighter moments, Fanny's day was tiring, the routine was dull, the work was menial, and freedom was practically non-existent. Although the Queen appears to have been genuinely fond of her, telling Mrs. Delany that she was difficult to know but well worth the trouble to befriend,[7] Charlotte was indifferent to Fanny's personal problems and oblivious of her physical condition.

Overlooking these matters, Fanny wrote favorably about the Queen. Whether motivated by loyalty or by personal affection, she has left a flattering portrait. It is well known, for example, that Charlotte had some difficulty in speaking English, having been reared and educated in Germany. When Fanny first met her, she wrote that her "accent is a little foreign" and "her language is rather peculiar." [8] The Queen's conversation in the *Diary*, how-

ever, is flawless both in structure and pronunciation, suggesting
that Fanny edited it. In addition, Fanny has nothing but praise
for the wisdom and intelligence of the Queen, qualities neither
apparent in her actions recorded in the *Diary* or in historical accounts. Here, as elsewhere, readers would welcome some candor.

Few personal details about the Queen are disclosed except for
her dislike of jewelry, her aversion to novels and most novelists,
and her love and affection for her children and the King. Similarly, Fanny reveals little about him. One may absolve her for this
omission because she had less opportunity to observe the King.
But she generally ignores his widely satirized speech mannerisms.
One realizes how much she has edited his conversations when she
expresses surprise at the King's reading on a formal occasion "with
ease, feeling, and force, and without any hesitation" in a voice
that was "particularly full and fine." Fanny does picture his genial
good-nature and sense of humor when teasing her about her skill
at fixing snuff for the Queen or about her blushing at compliments
paid her.

Fanny's account of the King's temporary insanity is historically
the most important section of the *Diary*. She portrays in detail the
growing apprehension about George's strange, wild, and irra-
tional conduct, the Queen's despondent lamentations; and the
doctors' increasing concern about their royal patient. Parliament
began discussing the Regency Bill, giving royal authority to the
profligate Prince of Wales, a favorite of Charles Fox and the opposition. The King rallied and relapsed, the doctors testified before Commons, the royal party's hopes ebbed and flowed, and the
Regency Bill drew nearer a vote. Thus the days passed from November, 1888, to February, 1889. Fanny's entry on February 2 began with the Evelina-like statement: "What an adventure had I
this morning! one that has occasioned me the severest personal
terror I ever experienced in my life." [9]

Then she related how she was walking in the garden when she
heard the King call out to her. Alarmed at his unexpected presence and aware of orders to avoid him, Fanny ran. He pursued
her with attendants and doctors after him. She wrote that nobody
would have caught her if she had not heard a shout about the
chase being detrimental to the King's health. After halting and
nervously allowing him to approach, Fanny was stunned to hear
him ask why she had fled. Without waiting for her answer, the

King, overjoyed at seeing a member of his household, placed his hands on Fanny's shoulders and kissed her cheek. This unusual conduct frightened her, but the accompanying doctors nodded reassuringly. Then the King walked with her, saying that "he was quite well—as well as he had ever been in his life" and telling her, among numerous other things, "I know you have a hard time of it" and "Stick to your father—stick to your family—let them be your objects." [10] Urged by his doctor to leave, the King promised that he would protect Fanny and be her friend; then he kissed her again and departed.

In a few weeks, the King was fully recovered; the Regency Bill was discarded by the House of Lords; and Fanny wrote, "Huzza! huzza," with a heart so full of joy and thankfulness that she could "hardly breathe." The King was his old self, teasing her by saying that he could catch her better now!

The description of the King's mental breakdown, the royal family's anxiety, the alternating hope and despair following favorable and unfavorable reports, the concern over the Regency Bill, and the tension created by the personal and national interest in the episode are graphically and dramatically depicted. Fanny had superb skill as a storyteller, and she had a superb story to tell. She used details effectively, created atmosphere, maintained suspense in building to the climax, and portrayed vividly the key scene, her conversation with the King. She not only shaped the material artistically but also edited it to protect the royal family from malicious gossip. Missing from her account is anything about the recovered King's refusal to see the Queen because he erroneously believed that she had deserted him earlier. Nor did Fanny mention anything about his wish to be with Lady Pembroke, or his extravagant gifts and promises to attendants and others around him. Whatever was unfavorable to the image of a happy and devoted King and Queen, kind and considerate to all, trusting and content with one another, was excluded here and elsewhere in the *Diary*.

Fanny's aversion to descriptive passages is waived in her detailed account of the jubilant reception given the King that spring and summer as he passed through numerous towns on his way to Weymouth.[11] Fanny concluded that "his popularity was greater than ever. Compassion for his late suffering seems to have endeared him to all conditions of men." At Winchester the town was

of *"one head."* Fanny was moved to tears when a band of common people dressed in "common brown coarse cloth and red neck-
cloths, and even in carters' loose gowns" sang "God Save the
King." This description of dress in her *Diary* is as unusual as her
listing of carriages lining the road: "chariots, chaises, landaus,
carts, waggons, whiskies, gigs, phaetons—mixed and intermixed,
filled with and surrounded without by faces all glee and delight."

Seldom in other sections of the *Diary* does Fanny seem aware
of scenery, sounds, clothes, colors, and objects. Here she believed
that because everything and everyone attested to the King's popularity, she should note it all. It was an indication of the people's
faith in their King, which needed reaffirmation after his illness
and after the hostile criticism received following the American
Revolution. In London the opposition had long been disparaging
the King. Here with the people she found such displays of love
and devotion that she wished to record everything.[12]

II *Trial Reporter*

Fanny's unswerving loyalty to the King and Queen is also evident in her account of the Hastings trial. Warren Hastings, like his
predecessor Robert Clive, had labored valiantly to establish English dominion in India and to bring order to the administrative
chaos there. England was greatly indebted to both men for their
remarkable work, although both had resorted at times to immoral
means to accomplish their ends. As if to salve its conscience, Parliament needed a scapegoat. Clive, severely censured, was there-
after found dead, probably a suicide. Fourteen years later, Hastings was impeached on twenty counts. The attack against him was
led by Burke, whose high moral sense would not condone inhumanity and injustice under any circumstances.

Fanny had met Warren Hastings years earlier, enjoyed listening to his stories about India, and been favorably impressed with
him. Sympathetic, therefore, both on personal and political
grounds (the Whig opposition was pressing the charges), her bias
is evident throughout her account. Fanny's meticulous record of
the trial's opening day is extensive but fails to convey the color,
pomp, and pageantry that Macaulay captured years later.[13] Her
description of the different galleries, the location of the various
participants and the prominent people, creates little awareness of
the dazzling spectacle or the grandeur of Westminster Hall.

Fanny's ear and memory were, however, superior to her eye; she retained so much of what was said that at one point she mentioned matter-of-factly that her account of Lord Thurlow's opening speech was more accurate than the newspaper's.

In the midst of the solemn and stirring proceedings, Fanny provided moments of humor. Good-naturedly she told about her Evelina-like perplexity at the cries of "Hear! hear! hear him!" and her embarrassment at being informed that this outburst was the customary sign of Parliament's approval. In a later passage, she recorded the remarks of a Commons member who might have appeared in any of her novels: "What a bore! when will it be over? —Must one come any more?—I had a great mind not to come at all.—Who's that? Lady Hawkesbury and the Copes?—Yes? A pretty girl, Kitty. Well, when will they have done? I wish they'd call the question.—I should vote it a bore at once!" [14]

The King and Queen evidently relied heavily on Fanny's account to them of the proceedings because they sent her to attend some twenty sessions of the trial that lasted over a seven-year period. Historians have recorded the event for posterity, but Fanny's account preserves the typical reaction of the time. She viewed Warren Hastings as a national hero who had brought peace and stability to India, thus securing English control. Like most people, Fanny was confused by the involved issues, the complicated charges, the contradictory evidence, and the irrelevant statements. Like most people, she viewed the trial as a political attempt to embarrass the government; she decided the case upon sentiment rather than evidence; and she was more concerned about the English hero being humiliated than about the Indian multitudes being oppressed. Her account of the trial is valuable, therefore, in suggesting why the final twenty-three to six verdict favoring Hastings was so one-sided despite the damaging facts revealed.

In addition, Fanny provides readers with a perceptive view of a major eighteenth-century figure, Edmund Burke. No one else has conveyed so vividly a picture of him as an orator. Although Fanny listened to him on several occasions, she never expressed anything but awe and admiration for his forensic ability. She noted his faults, she violently opposed what he said, but she admired his ability and recognized him as the leader of the opposition. Although unable or unwilling to comprehend his argument, she real-

ized that he was guided by a deep and sincere conviction. To
Fanny as to others, the drama was provided at the trial whenever
Burke rose to speak. All paid rapt attention as the great statesman
held forth eloquently and passionately, declaiming his noble ethi-
cal principles that caused him to seek justice for all, in all English
dominions, and under all circumstances. Burke was far ahead of
his age; England had not yet developed a conscience. But Fanny
was very much of her age. Although her account is personal not
factual, dramatic not pictorial, prejudiced not objective, and
sketchy not complete, it is vivid, interesting, and informative for
the light it sheds on the proceedings, the personages, and the period.

III *Unrequited Love*

While the journal of the court years is richer than any other
section of the *Diary* in describing historical events and in discussing political figures, it contains its share of personal observations
and episodes. There are such highly exciting accounts as the one
of Fanny getting lost one evening while being carried from the
ballroom to her apartment by drunk and belligerent chairmen.
Only the assistance of an unknown clergyman summoned by
Fanny's screams averted a more unpleasant evening. Less exciting
but equally diverting are her social dilemmas. Among these are
such contretemps as whether to correspond with the brilliant, admiring, but notorious Mme Genlis (the Queen advised against it);
how to avoid inviting the officious Mme de la Fite, and her author
friend, Mme de la Roche, to dinner when they were pointedly
waiting (Fanny finally admitted frankly that she could not have
guests); and what to do about her servant, John, who composed
and delivered fictitious messages inviting Fanny to visit the equerries or vice versa (she embarrassedly revealed everything to them
and cashiered John).

Although Fanny enjoyed the friendship of many equerries and
men at court, two in particular play a large role in the *Diary*. One,
called Mr. Turbulent, was actually Reverend Charles de Guiffar-
diere, a French Protestant clergyman who tutored the princesses
and read to Queen Charlotte. He was an unpredictable, argumentative man, who derived enjoyment by annoying people. Fanny
was constantly unsettled by his queries, upset by his strange
whims, confused by his ardent protestations of friendship, dis-

tressed by his misanthropic views, and bewildered by his informality and daring with the royal family. Whenever he appears,
whether to disconcert Fanny or to nettle someone else, there is not
a dull moment. Fanny found him annoying and entertaining,
varying her opinion from complete dislike to reluctant admiration.
Few of her fictional eccentrics are as well portrayed as this singular gentleman who was consistently inconsistent and who derived
great pleasure from quarreling and being quarreled with.

Another man of great interest is a widower, Mr. Fairly, the
pseudonym for Colonel Stephen Digby, the Queen's vice-
chamberlain. Fanny was originally attracted to him by his delicacy, sensitivity, learning, and decorum. No one could have been
more attentive to her than Fairly; indeed, no one had ever been so
intensely concerned about her spiritual, intellectual, and personal
well-being as he. Fanny and Fairly spent hours together reading
sermons, sentimental poems, and collections, such as *Original
Love Letters*. Nothing kept him from visiting her. Even when
confined with gout, he defied doctor's orders and turned up at
her apartment, walking with a stick and in a gouty shoe. He
schemed how to be with her more often, asking, for example, to
be permitted to write letters in her parlor because his desk was
uncomfortable. Sometimes he remained after others left so that he
could see her alone.

Now thirty six, Fanny must have realized that she could not be
as discreet and circumspect as formerly. Marital opportunities in
the seclusion of court life were minimal. Mr. Fairly was "a highly
cultivated" gentleman with "the tenderest social affections," "the
most acute sensibility," and "a high moral character." Fanny knew
that she had neither social position nor fortune to attract him. Yet
her discussions with him were so personal, his enjoyment of her
company was so apparent, and their time together was so serene
that she had high expectations.

In fiction, Fanny's heroines always landed their men; in life,
Fanny did not. Jeremiah Crutchley and George Cambridge never
proposed to her; neither did Mr. Fairly who turned instead to the
attractive, wealthy Miss Fuzilier (actually Miss Gunning). Fanny
could not forget Fairly, but she derived some consolation from
hearing that his wedding was held in a private home under make-
shift circumstances. Then she realized that there was more to this
man than she had known. How could he "with so little solemnity

—without even a room prepared and empty—to go through a
business of such portentous seriousness!" [15] Such conduct was
"amazing from a man who seemed to delight in religious regula-
tions and observations."

IV   The Tragedy of the Tragedies

Fanny turned from her own tragedy to the writing of them. The
first, *Edwy and Elgiva*,[16] is a heroic, blank verse play based upon
David Hume's account of the tenth-century West Saxon conflict
between King Eadwig and the English monks over his marriage
to Aelgifu. In Fanny's play, King Edwy and his distant cousin
Elgiva, already secretly married, find their formal wedding plans
blocked by Dunstan, Abbot of Glastonbury, and other Church fa-
thers because canon law prohibits a union between relatives. During the ensuing struggle between forces of Church and State,
Dunstan abducts Elgiva. She escapes, and returns to Edwy, who
exiles Dunstan. This action results in a revolt against the King, the
murder of Elgiva, and finally the killing of Edwy.

Fanny's play has strong anti-Catholic elements in revealing the
corrupt and cruel power of the Pope and his representatives in
forbidding King Edwy to marry, in passing a sentence of divorce
upon the revealed marriage, and in excommunicating Elgiva for
her actions. But *Edwy and Elgiva* is not mainly concerned with
the clash between Church and State. Instead, the play deals with
the attempt of the diabolical Dunstan to gain power by turning
the nobles against the King and by persuading the weak Edgar to
lead the revolt against his brother Edwy. The Abbot's machinations are directed against the innocence, sweetness, and purity of
the young lovers. Aldhelm, the King's wise advisor (a typical Burney mentor character), states that inexperience and credulity can
not withstand evil in this world, although they will be rewarded in
the next. This bleak message of Christian resignation echoes the
ending of *Cecilia* and expresses Fanny's mood resulting from her
disappointing experience with Fairly, and from her general unhappiness at court.

Two other thematic ideas might well have been derived from
Fanny's experiences at the time. The wise Aldhelm expounds at
length about the arduous task of being king, particularly singling
out the mental strains resulting from the need to subordinate personal problems to national ones. Writing these lines shortly after

George III's breakdown, Fanny undoubtedly had him in mind and may well have equated the hostile Catholic leaders with the opposition party of Fox, Sheridan, and Burke; and the treacherous brother Edgar with the English counterpart, the Prince of Wales. Besides this political similarity, the parallel is striking between Edwy's desire to marry for love rather than money or position, and Fanny's hope that Fairly felt similarly towards her. As already noted, this romantic concept was an essential part of Fanny's dream world, where gentlemen attracted to her person would not be repelled by her lack of dowry or social rank.

Edwy and Elgiva with its ideological conflict, dramatic scenes, tender love story, and exciting action is a suitable vehicle for a successful tragedy. But Fanny's ability to write eloquent and stirring poetry was limited, and the lines fail to rouse or affect the reader. In portraying the passions of love, hate, anger, and jealousy, the language moves from bathos to bombast. As a result of the verbal and metrical deficiencies of the poetry, the characters sound grandiloquent instead of grandiose, and insipid instead of inspiring. Their weakness is further augmented by Fanny's failure to develop them with any degree of complexity or depth; only Edwy, as a result of his rashness and petulance, achieves any human dimension. Other major weaknesses in the play are the protracted death of Elgiva, lasting for some twenty minutes; the repetition of her abduction; the lack of action and slow pace in the last two acts; and Dunstan's hasty repentance at the play's end.

But *Edwy and Elgiva* is not without some merit. Occasionally Fanny writes powerful lines, and in several places she rises to dramatic intensity without rant. Several scenes are well-developed. In one, Aldhelm tries to convince the assembled lords and priests to accept Elgiva as the princess. In another, Edwy, deeply upset by the abduction of his wife, gradually loses control of himself, and wildly banishes Dunstan. In these scenes and a few others, the action grows out of the interplay between characters. Elsewhere, extravagance and sensationalism dominate the plot and dictate its direction.

This same weakness is noticeable in *Hubert de Vere*,[17] subtitled *A Pastoral Tragedy* but more of a Gothic romance than anything else. Among other things, the complicated plot involves treason, blackmail, madness, and suicide attempts against a background of deserted heaths, desolate graveyards, and supernatural events.

The sentimental hero De Vere is exiled to the Isle of Wight and betrayed by his love, "the false Geralda." In exile, he meets the innocent, artless Cerulia; falls in love with her; but repents when the widowed Geralda appears, explaining that she was forced to marry another to save her uncle, De Mowbray. Then he turns up on the island and discloses that he tricked Geralda into marrying, caused De Vere to be falsely exiled, and also brought about the romance between De Vere and Cerulia. After each woman unselfishly offers De Vere to the other, Cerulia reveals that she is dying. At this moment, De Mowbray enters, announces that she is his daughter, and that he has killed her by breaking her heart. After De Vere prevents De Mowbray from committing suicide, a messenger enters to bring both men back to England; the hero is to be honored and the villain imprisoned.

With its melodramatic plot, excessive sentimentality, unmotivated villain, and rhetorically swollen lines, *Hubert de Vere* has little literary merit. The characterization of Cerulia captures some of the sweetness and freshness of Evelina early in the play but her later account of the church graveyard, where a white vision leads her to measure out her own grave, and her actions during a lingering death scene spoil her portrayal.

The play is interesting, however, as a forerunner of Fanny's Gothic-like novel, *The Wanderer;* as an example of her ability to use natural settings occasionally for dramatic effect; and as another vehicle deploring the marriage of convenience. One can hear Fanny's voice in De Vere's sarcastic remark to Geralda: "A proud alliance with a richer husband, / A true, true woman's motive." [18] Fanny may also have been expressing her own disillusionment in dying Cerulia's lines about the life hereafter "where guileful hopes no more deceive" and "sorrow breaks the heart no more." [19]

A later play, *The Siege of Pevensey*,[20] is similar to heroic drama in its conflict of love and duty. Fanny departs from the tradition, however, by adding a happy ending, some chauvinistic lines honoring the "Patriot King," and a comic character, Mowbray. The plot deals with a series of crises arising from the capture of Adela, daughter of the Duke of Chester, by his enemy, Robert de Belesme. When the prisoner and her captor fall in love, one problem in the play is posed: should Adela marry without her father's permission in view of her being in love and of her being forced to marry another if she does not wed De Belesme? Chester arrives in disguise; lectures her on filial obedience; and, aided by De Belesme, escapes with her to their lines. When De Belesme is captured, Chester is suspected of disloyalty. Sentenced to death, he is promised a reprieve if his daughter marries the detestable De Warrenne. He prefers death to compelling his daughter to wed; she protests, unwilling to be responsible for his death. Seeking a compromise, she requests permission to go to a convent, and receives it. Fanny should have let matters end unhappily at that point; instead, she brought about peace between the opposing forces just in time to save De Belesme's life and allow him to marry Adela.

Because the conflicts result from the basic situation of the siege, and from the interaction of characters rather than the machinations of a diabolical villain, the plot is superior to those in the other tragedies. In addition, the action is sustained throughout instead of being unevenly distributed as in *Edwy and Elgiva*. Finally, the verse is less objectionable although it is thin and contributes little to the emotional effect.

Once again Fanny was concerned mainly with marriage, particularly with a daughter's obligation to her father, and his to her. The play suggests that a daughter should obey her father, but that he should never force her to marry against her will. The biographical implications of this thematic idea are apparent when one recalls that Fanny equated her court service with marriage. Writing the play during her unhappy days in the royal household, she may well be speaking out against the father who compelled her to accept the Queen's offer.

A fourth tragedy, *Elberta*,[21] exists only in a preliminary form. The list of characters, sketches of them, plot ideas, fragments of dialogue, and outline of scenes are interesting indications of how Fanny worked. Despite an ingenious and imaginative construction of the play by Morrison,[22] *Elberta* might best be forgotten because of its incompleteness and because of the highly melodramatic nature of the existing fragments.

Fanny's tragedies, like most of those in the eighteenth century, may be disregarded by all except the specialist. Her three completed plays contain little literary value. While they provided her with a therapeutic release for her frustrations, occupied her time, and gave her additional experience in writing dramas, they are interesting to readers mainly for the light they shed on her personal problems and for their foreshadowing of *The Wanderer.*

V   *Escape from Tyranny*

Fanny presented the tragedy in her own life more effectively than she depicted the plight of her dramatic heroines. *The Diary* reveals how she endured the maliciousness of Mrs. Schwellenberg, the First Keeper of the Robes, by escaping to visit Mrs. Delany during the early days at court. After Mrs. Delany's death, Mrs. Schwellenberg grew more demanding. To avoid unpleasantness, Fanny became more conciliatory. She learned how to play cards and pique for Mrs. Schwellenberg's sake. She was quiet during dinner so as not to detract from the attention that the older woman craved. She did everything possible to anticipate controversy and to avoid it; but all for naught. Mrs. Schwellenberg grew more jealous as Fanny became more cherished by the royal family. The situation was intolerable.

Fanny stoically endured her plight until she began to suffer from the same illness that had caused her predecessor, Mrs. Haggerdorn, to retire and return to Germany. This malady, an eye inflamation caused by a heavy cold, resulted from Mrs. Schwellenberg's callous insistence that the window next to Fanny be kept open during coach rides despite the freezing weather. Fanny realized the seriousness of her illness when Mrs. Miller, the old head housemaid, brought her milk with butter, just as she had previously done with Mrs. Haggerdorn, who had nearly gone blind.

The physical hardships, the indignities suffered from the tyrannical Mrs. Schwellenberg, the fatigue of duties, and the oppressiveness of confinement gradually wore Fanny down. Finally, "half dead with real illness" but strengthened by her father's consent, she presented her resignation to the Queen. Eventually Charlotte, realizing the seriousness of Fanny's condition, sent to Germany for a replacement.

Like an accomplished playwright, Fanny closed the curtain on these court years with a dramatic scene.[23] The Queen, who had given Fanny a life pension of a hundred pounds, requested her assistance for the last time. While Fanny was helping her, the King came in. Realizing that Fanny was so overcome by sentiment that she was unable to face him, he walked away rather than force her to confront him. Then Fanny "took for the last time, the cloak of the Queen, and, putting it over her shoulders," stated in a low voice, "God Almighty bless your Majesty!" The Queen responded by holding Fanny's hand and wishing her happiness. The three eldest princesses entered, crowded around the emotionally overwhelmed Fanny, and repeated over and over again, "I wish you happy!—I wish you health!" Then they departed for Kew, while Fanny left for the freedom of private life.

CHAPTER 7

A Husband, a Child, and a Novel!

AFTER a rest, Fanny celebrated her release from court life by traveling leisurely with Mrs. Ord through Farnham to Sidmouth, and then on to Bath. There they heard about Burke's blaming the Queen for Fanny's hard treatment. Writing to Dr. Burney, the diarist exonerates Charlotte by explaining that no one could have foreseen "the subserviency expected, so unjustly and unwarrantably by Mrs. Schwellenberg." [1] Fanny is generous to a fault because the Queen should have been aware of the arduous situation from the condition of Fanny's predecessor or from the deterioration of Fanny's health that was apparent to all.

After returning from Bath, Fanny by chance met Boswell, whom she disliked for publishing the *Life* without expunging Johnson's faults and weaknesses. "How many starts of passion and prejudices has he [Boswell] blackened into record, that might else have sunk forever forgotten, under the preponderance of weightier virtues and excellencies." [2] Despite her coolness, Boswell cleverly "conquered, though he did not soften" Fanny. Yet she confessed that they parted "good friends." How he managed to overcome Fanny's aversion would have been interesting to read, but she evidently did not believe him important enough to write about at greater length.

At the home of Mrs. Crewe, a magnificent beauty who "uglifies everything near her," Fanny encountered another old friend, Edmund Burke. At first somewhat cool towards him because of his speeches against Hastings, Fanny soon was enthralled by his animated conversation and by his strong statements supporting monarchy. Referring to him as "the very first man of true genius now living in this country," she stated that he made "the day delicious" for her. Part of her reaction was due to Burke's publication of *Reflections on the French Revolution,* for she had been concerned for almost the first time with international affairs upon learning about the catastrophic events in France. At the time, Burke seemed to be the only public leader aware of the serious threat that the revolution posed to England's political and social order.

Fanny applauded his passionate pronouncements and eloquent statements. She had met and admired several emigrants, particularly the fascinating Duc de Liancourt. In addition, Susan was writing at length about the French refugees at Juniper Hall who told touching tales of distress and suffering. Like Susan, Burke, and many others, Fanny was unaware of tyranny of the *ancien regime* or the plight of the French populace.

I *The Charming Frenchman*

Soon Susan was writing about a new arrival, M. d'Arblay, former adjutant-general to Lafayette during his campaign against the Prussians. About forty, d'Arblay was personally attractive, intelligent, and good-natured. Added to these attributes was the romantic glamor of his close friendship with the famous Frenchman and of his own thrilling escape from prison. Susan was quite taken with him. Whether she was interested in matchmaking is problematical, but her letters were filled with praises of him, and once she included one of his speeches. Fanny was impressed with it, urging that it be translated and read "to all English imitators of French reformers."

In due time, Fanny visited Susan and found d'Arblay to be "one of the most delightful characters I have ever met, for openness, probity, intellectual knowledge, and unhackneyed manners." [3] A later letter refers to him as "most singularly interesting" with "a sincerity, a frankness, and ingenuous openness of nature" unlike anything that Fanny felt could belong to a Frenchman. She also discovered him to be "passionately fond" of literature, an "elegant poet," a discerning critic, and fluent in both Italian and German.

Under other circumstances Dr. Burney might have been concerned about Fanny's daily French lessons with the attractive *émigré*. However, he did not appear apprehensive about her becoming romantically involved. After all, Fanny was forty, past the age when most women married, and d'Arblay was a penniless Roman Catholic foreigner without any means of support. Besides, Dr. Burney was disturbed about something else: his daughter's association with the notorious Madame de Staël. When he urged Fanny not to visit her as had been planned, Fanny replied with a strong and detailed defense of Madame de Staël, expressing scorn and astonishment at "the acrimony of malice" and stating that the Frenchwoman was deserving of "honour, compassion, and praise." Because of Fanny's association with the Queen, however, she was reluctant to become involved with any controversial person. Consequently, although writing that she was "vexed, very much vexed" and wishing that "the world would take more care of itself, and less of its neighbours," [4] she complied with her father's wishes.

It may have been that Fanny was willing to lose the skirmish in order to win the following battle. Although it is impossible to know exactly when Fanny realized the seriousness of her regard for d'Arblay, it may have been about this time. The impersonal *Diary,* unlike a confession, does not reveal Fanny's moments of awakening, doubting, despairing, hoping, planning, and deciding. Even the unpublished account of her courtship,[5] which is delightfully satirical rather than sentimentally serious, discloses little about her attitudes and reactions during this trying period.

The obstacles in the way of her marrying d'Arblay were formidable. Fanny had dealt with the *mésalliance* problem in *Cecilia,* but there, as in her next novel, *Camilla,* the heroine's fiancé was socially above her. A woman's marrying beneath her was questionable because it suggested a strong sexual desire that no respectable woman, especially one about forty, should admit to. For that reason, society had frowned upon Mrs. Thrale; now it was gossiping about Fanny even though there were mitigating circumstances. Unlike Mrs. Thrale, Fanny had neither children nor wealth; and, unlike Piozzi, d'Arblay was socially acceptable, particularly under normal times in his own country. Yet despite these differences, Fanny's unconventional marriage necessitated daring and determination.

Dr. Burney was not easily overcome. When he first had wind of the affair, he wrote to "beg, warn, and admonish" Fanny against "a wild and romantic attachment, which offers nothing in prospect but poverty and distress, with future inconvenience and unhappiness." The practical Dr. Burney pointed out that d'Arblay had no money, little chance of obtaining any from France, and almost no opportunity of finding "an establishment" in England. In strong language, he implored, "For Heaven's sake, my dear Fanny, do not part with your heart too rapidly or invoke yourself in deep engagements which it will be difficult to dissolve." [6]

Dr. Burney also questioned whether the Queen would continue Fanny's annual pension if she married a Catholic foreigner. Fanny had anticipated this problem by having a friend at court sound out Charlotte. Much to the credit of the Queen, she ignored unfavorable rumors about Fanny and stated that she would not terminate the pension. With this one hundred pounds and an annual annuity payment of twenty pounds from *Cecilia*'s profits, Fanny believed that she could live modestly, for many country curates managed on the same income (about $2,400 today). Because Fanny's needs had always been simple, she felt that she would be happy with "a crust of bread, with a little roof for shelter, and a fire for warmth." As for d'Arblay, he required only "le simple necessaire."

If Fanny had written a novel about herself and d'Arblay, it would have gone on for several volumes with sentimental scenes, eccentric characters, and the fortunes of the hero and heroine rising and falling until parental consent was forthcoming. In reality, Fanny, probably with Susan's help, soon overcame Dr. Burney's opposition to the union but evidently did not obtain his approval because he failed to attend the wedding. Taking her father's place at St. Michael's Church in Mickleham on July 28, 1793, was Captain James Burney. The ceremony was repeated two days later at a Catholic chapel in London so that Fanny would be recognized as d'Arblay's legal wife if they ever returned to France.

The *Diary* account of Fanny's involved love affair is disappointing. The absence of information may be attributed in part to her being with Susan and Mrs. Locke during most of the courtship, thus having no need of an epistolary confidant; and in part to her withholding some of the material from publication. What remains is interesting and humorous but fails to do justice to the courage and conviction required of the forty-one-year-old author in persevering with her plans to marry a man reared in a different faith, in a different country, and in a different social system. For personal reasons, Fanny chose not to write any details about the most fecund situation that she had experienced.

II *Living on Love*

The couple soon moved from their first quarters at Phenice
Farm about a mile from Brookham, to a comfortable cottage at
Fairfield Place, where they were within walking distance of Susan, the Lockes, and other friends. Here d'Arblay assiduously cultivated his garden while Fanny busied herself with domestic
affairs or wrote amusingly about his efforts. Once the general labored in clearing away a plot of weeds only to discover that they
were asparagus. Another time he transplanted strawberries without realizing that they would not bear fruit the following year.

As for herself, Fanny enjoyed the "tranquil, undisturbed, and
undisturbing" life. While she did her needlework, d'Arblay read
to her. Often they took "long and romantic strolls" in the beautiful
countryside. In such a fashion—reading, walking, gardening, visiting friends, and writing letters—the d'Arblays passed their first
year of married life. It was, as Fanny wrote, "A year that has not
been blemished with one regretful moment." [7]

Nor was this euphoria broken more than once or twice in the
next few years. The production of her tragedy, *Edwy and Elgiva,*
was one such occasion. What caused her to permit its being
staged was the success of her pamphlet, *Brief Reflections relative
to the Emigrant French Clergy,* written at the behest of her father
and Mrs. Crewe, who were distressed at the destitution of these
impoverished individuals. Fanny's twenty-seven page tribute in
flowing rhetoric to feminine benevolence was highly praised by
critics. They welcomed her return to literature and urged her to
"write on." Encouraged by this approbation, by her father's superlatives, and by the huge sale of the pamphlet, Fanny permitted
Charles to show her tragedy to Sheridan, although she had intended "divers corrections and alterations."

Fanny had nothing to do with the play from that time until she
attended its opening night performance on March 21, 1795, at the
Drury Lane Theatre. To her embarrassment, *Edwy and Elgiva*
was practically laughed off the stage because of its weaknesses
and the cast's poor acting. Fanny publicly withdrew the play for
revision; privately, she bemoaned her failure to attend rehearsals
where she might have rewritten the poorer scenes and required
the actors to know their lines. She wrote bitterly that, except for
Mrs. Siddons, Mr. Kemble, and Mr. Bensley, "a more wretched

performance could not be exhibited in a barn." [8] On the other hand, Mrs. Siddons commented that never was there "so wretched a thing as Mrs. d'Arblay's Tragedy" and that she regretted that a woman "of so much merit must be so mortified" in public.[9]

Fanny turned to more rewarding projects. First and foremost of these was taking care of her son Alex, whose birth had severely strained her health. For over ten weeks, the forty-two-year-old Fanny was confined in critical condition. When she recovered, she absorbed herself in her son. As she doted over him day after day, Fanny became more concerned about her parental responsibilities. No longer could she blissfully meet each month and year as it came; instead, she worried about the future for her "Bambino."

III Back to Work

That future seemed anything but secure. The war with France had brought increased taxes and inflationary pressures. The cost of living was rising steadily, prices having doubled during Fanny's first year and a half of housekeeping. Despite her economizing, and some assistance from her father, she found that living with only a few comforts was difficult. Under the circumstances, Fanny turned to "a long work, which a long time has been in hand." She had prepared "the skeleton" of it while in the royal service; now she struggled bringing it to life. During this time her family and friends found three hundred people willing to subscribe for *Camilla* at a guinea and a half each.

The list is impressive with its dukes and duchesses, its statesmen, and its literary figures, such as David Hume, Miss Radcliffe, and the then obscure Jane Austen. More pleasing to Fanny than these tributes was the permission granted by the Queen to dedicate the book to her. Not only was this consent an expression of her approval and recognition but it was also an endorsement of *Camilla*. Now the book could be read in the best of homes and by even the most sheltered girls because the royal family (excluding the sons) was known for its prudish views, and would place its seal of approval only on a moral work.

With the subscription by such illustrious individuals and with its dedication to the Queen, the new novel from the author of *Evelina* and *Cecilia* was destined for success. Shortly after it appeared on June 28, 1796, the first printing of *Camilla* was sold out. Although somewhat disappointed at its reviews, Fanny was comforted by the popular acclaim and the huge profits, amounting to about two thousand pounds (approximately forty thousand dollars). To her husband, her father, her family, her friends, and herself, *Camilla* was an important and significant work; to most critics—past and present—it was and is little more than a name in the Fanny Burney canon.[10]

IV *The Follies of Innocence*

Camilla is another version of *Cecilia* but on a larger, more diffuse canvas. The situation is the same: a young heroine is separated from the man who loves her due to misunderstandings, misinterpretations, fortuitous circumstances, and her own indiscretions. At the novel's end, after hovering close to death, she recovers and is happily united with him. Also similar is the theme: lack of worldly knowledge about people and money will result in distress to virtuous, innocent young ladies.

Although Fanny has followed the general outline of her previous work, she has constructed a superior plot but not a better novel. Her story revolves primarily around Camilla's romance with Edgar Mandlebert, but integrated with it are subplots dealing with her sister Eugenia, her brother Lionel, and her cousin Indiana. Subtitled *A Picture of Youth,* the novel portrays all these young people in various circumstances. Each is involved in a different type of problem, but one related to the central theme.

The main plot is superior to that in *Cecilia* because no such artificial device as the unusual clause in the will keeps the lovers apart. What prevents Edgar and Cecilia from marrying is a series of actions and interactions precipitated by others and complicated by the heroine's thoughtlessness and inexperience. However, the first stage of the love affair involves Indiana, who has been designated by Sir Hugh Tybold, the girls' wealthy uncle, as Edgar's wife. With her interest in Edgar whetted by his new carriage and his vast estate, and by the designing aspirations of her governess, Miss Margland, the beautiful but shallow Indiana plans to marry him. When he displays more concern for Camilla than for her, Indiana, as well as Miss Margland, accuses the heroine of trying to lure Edgar away. The tension increases with much soul-searching on Camilla's part until Edgar reveals his lack of interest in Indiana when questioned by one of her admirers.

The second stage of the romance deals with Edgar's watching

Camilla carefully to determine whether she loves him, and what
kind of wife she will make. He has been urged not to declare his
affection by his mentor, Dr. Marchmont, who has twice married
unhappily. While Edgar closely scrutinizes Camilla's conduct and
character, she becomes concerned at his failure to indicate his love.
On the advice of her mentor, Mrs. Arlbery, an older, sophisticated
nonconformist, Camilla permits Sir Sedley Clarendal to escort her
to places. Their friendship develops as the wealthy Sir Sedley provides her with tickets, buys her an expensive bullfinch, loans her
brother two hundred pounds, and plies her with favors. Just as Sir
Sedley is about to ask for her hand, Edgar discovers that Camilla
truly cares for him when she is frightened at the possibility of his
being hurt at a dog fight. The lovers meet alone, explain their
misunderstandings, and plan their marriage.

A happy ending at this point might suggest that Fanny ap-
proves of Camilla's flirtation. To avoid this interpretation, Camilla
must suffer. Stage three of the novel, therefore, drops the heroine
from the previous heights to the nadir of despair. It begins auspi-
ciously with Edgar bursting into Camilla's room when she screams
as Sir Sedley tries to kiss her hand. Why Edgar was present at
Mrs. Arlbery's house at the time is not well accounted for, nor is
his leaving without asking Camilla for any explanation.

Added complications develop soon afterwards because Camilla
is first mistaken for a shoplifter and then for a prostitute while
walking around Southampton with Mrs. Mittin. As an outcome
of this humiliating misunderstanding and its almost distressing
consequences, which Edgar forestalls by arriving unexpectedly at
the climactic moment, Camilla almost causes a duel, but again
Edgar saves the day. Next Camilla is courted by Mr. Westwin, Jr.
When he becomes seriously interested in her, she turns to his father. Then to deter Mr. Westwin's advances, she directs her attention to the suave Lord Valhurst. Edgar not only disapproves of
these male attachments but also of her female companions, particularly the beautiful but highly romantic Mrs. Berlinton, who in-
stalled a faro table in her house and has been meeting clandestinely with a married man.

About this time, other events begin to plague Camilla. Her inability to repay the money borrowed from Clykes, a money-lender,
causes her father to be sent to jail. Her cousin Indiana, although
engaged to Melmond, runs off with Macderfy. Her sister Eu-

genia suffers daily punishment and humiliation from the abominable Bellamy, whom she was tricked into marrying. Camilla's parents appear to have rejected her for her improprieties. Overwhelmed, distraught, ill, and despairing of help, Camilla sits alone in an inn waiting for death and writing final letters to Edgar and her parents. A sudden contrived reversal of fortune brings about the happy ending when Bellamy accidentally shoots himself; and Edgar, disguised as a clergyman, listens to Camilla declare her love for him. Then her parents, whose letter of forgiveness had gone astray, arrive to welcome her back into the fold.

What mainly spoils the Edgar-Camilla love story is its tediousness and the dullness of the participants. Early in the novel, Edgar consults Dr. Marchmont about marrying Camilla; some 1,860 pages later he proposes to her. Admittedly, some of the delay is justified in terms of Camilla's flirting with other men. Much of it, however, is due to endless misunderstandings and misinterpretations that are not clarified because Fanny seldom allowed the lovers to meet alone. Occasionally, when the situation became overwhelmingly intricate and involved, Edgar and Camilla were brought together to straighten matters out temporarily, but different complications soon arose, and interminable difficulties piled up anew. Camilla is not the only one exhausted and weary at the novel's end.

The drawing out of the plot to such an untenable length might have been bearable if the main characters had been more interesting. Both, however, are bland, lifeless individuals. Neither has a sense of humor, a spark of eccentricity, a keenness of perception, a vivaciousness of speech, or any other trait to suggest individuality. Edgar talks in the same stilted, pompous, affected language of Lord Orville and Mortimer Delvile; and seldom does he sound like a human being. Camilla is often more natural, especially in scenes with her brother Lionel; but she never appears interesting enough to attract numerous admirers or readers.

Although lacking in individuality, Camilla is at least not the perfect heroine. Her troubles, in fact, develop mainly from impetuously accepting the advice of Mrs. Arlbery, the help of Miss Mifflin, the friendship of Mrs. Berlinton, the entreaties of Lionel, and the loan from Clykes. All of these people serve to undo her and to exemplify how innate goodness and innocence can be led astray. Camilla's weakness, often referred to as "wayward Sensibility," negates the judgment and causes a person to be misdirected by "the ardour of . . . [the] imagination." [11] Camilla's occasional faintings, her many tears, her kindness to animals, and her benevolence to the poor are positive virtues, or demonstrations of a proper sensibility.

Excessiveness is revealed in some of Camilla's follies but mainly in the actions of Mrs. Berlinton and her brother Melmond. First encountered in a rapturous state while reading Thomson's "Seasons" aloud to himself, Melmond loses most of his sentimental inclinations as he gradually becomes disillusioned with his idealized Indiana ("that divinity"). At the novel's end, he has learned to control his imaginative flights and to rely more on his reason. His sister, Mrs. Berlinton, comes to no such self-discovery. Like her brother, she is first introduced to readers in an exotic manner. Wandering alone on a moonlight night in the country, dressed in white and reading aloud a letter, Mrs. Berlinton believes that Camilla is "a pitying Angel" mercifully come to her rescue. But nothing can help Mrs. Berlinton, who soon engages in an illicit affair and also establishes gambling in her house. The dangers of a romantic sensibility are apparent.

V *Guidelines for Parents*

The subplot involving Camilla's sister Eugenia reinforces the idea that inexperienced innocence is helpless and that a romantic heart is dangerous. Eugenia, a deformed cripple, had followed her uncle's wishes by studying the classics to prepare herself for marrying his nephew, Clermont, who was at school abroad. When he returned, contrary to expectation, he refused to marry her. Disillusioned and disappointed, Eugenia fell in love with the sentimental, handsome Melmond. After their engagement, however, she overheard him declare his affection for Indiana. Realizing that his poverty prevented him from marrying this woman, Eugenia magnanimously broke her engagement to him and gave Melmond half of her own inheritance.

At this point Eugenia was ripe for Bellamy, who had ardently approached her upon several occasions. In the tradition of Lovelace and other rakes, Bellamy abducted her and threatened to kill himself (shades of Harrel and Cecilia!) if she didn't marry him; thus he became her husband. Even though he is soon revealed to be a notorious blackguard, Eugenia refuses to renounce her wedding vows by leaving him, or to face the publicity of a court trial by pleading marriage under duress. Unbelievably, she suffers and endures beatings and cruelty in order to prove Fanny's contention that greater parental supervision might have spared this example of "innocence oppressed through its own artlessness, and inexperience duped by villainy." [12]

Besides reinforcing this lesson of the central plot, Eugenia illustrates another thematic concept. Deformed and crippled at eight after falling out of a tree, and scarred from smallpox shortly afterwards, Eugenia is supposedly unaware of her physical repulsiveness until Dubster and others refer to it seven years later. Then the pockmarked, hunchbacked, lame midget bemoans having been sheltered from the truth, decides to withdraw from the world, and refuses to see outsiders. Her father arrives to preach and teach the lesson that beauty is a transitory, superficial quality that is of little value compared with intelligence and virtue. He provides proof by taking Eugenia to visit some poor children, who fawn over her when she gives them coins, but who ignore the lovely Camilla when she does not. Having indicated that popularity is simple and easy to achieve, Mr. Tyrold next brings her to view a beautiful woman who is wildly insane. Eugenia's statement indicates that she has learned the lesson well: "I will think of her when I am discontented . . . and submit, at least with calmness, to my lighter evils and milder fate." [13]

The subplot involving Indiana supplements the lesson. A beautiful but self-centered and fatuous girl, she lacks the intelligence and integrity of Eugenia and Camilla. In an early series of episodes, Indiana reveals her true nature. She sulks at Sir Hugh's decision to compensate for Eugenia's deformity by making her his heir; but Camilla graciously accepts the decision as only fitting and proper. Indiana feigns tears to avoid studying Latin, which she is too stupid to master, while Eugenia good-naturedly agrees to replace her and does well. And Indiana shows neither pity for nor the slightest interest in the poor petitioners, while Edgar and Camilla do everything possible for them.

Having established Indiana's character dramatically in this fashion, as well as directly in expository paragraphs, Fanny proceeds to illustrate how men are led astray by beauty. Edgar naturally sees behind Indiana's fair face; Melmond is not so perceptive. When Eugenia offers to break their engagement and subsidize his marriage to Indiana, he is overjoyed. He soon learned, however, that "his goddess had every mortal imperfection," was interested only in flattery, and had neither the ability to understand him nor the desire to make the effort. Regretfully he thought of Eugenia: "The purity of her love, the cultivation of her mind, and the nobleness of her sentiments, now bore a contrast to the general mental and intellectual littleness of Indiana." [14] Melmond profits from his experience; at the novel's end he returns to Eugenia after Indiana has run off with Macderfy.

VI *Several Shortcomings*

The black and white treatment of Eugenia and Indiana in order to disparage the attractiveness of beauty and to laud the merit of virtue is inartistically contrived. One would welcome a touch of jealousy or resentment in Eugenia, or a semblance of concern for others in Indiana. Without such shadings, without a more realistic ending than Melmond's returning to marry Eugenia, and without some growth and development in the characters, these subplots contribute little to the novel.

Another artistic weakness is Fanny's heavy reliance on coincidence, which has already been referred to and which had previously marred *Evelina* and *Cecilia*. The formula is the same: at precisely the most inopportune moment the ubiquitous hero encounters the heroine. For example, whenever Edgar advises Camilla against going somewhere or visiting someone, the reader knows that she will be forced to do so, and that Edgar will discover by chance that she has disregarded his instructions. Of course, a few words from Camilla might have explained the situation, but Edgar never gives her an opportunity, usually stalking off, thinking the worst. And so the novel plods tediously on and on.

Perhaps the use of this formula to perpetuate the plot might have been less objectionable if Fanny had not also fatigued her readers with lengthy didactic digressions. Not only is the story obviously contrived to reward virtue and punish vice, but huge segments of the novel's five volumes are devoted to overt moralizing. Included is an eighteen-page letter from Mr. Tyrold exhorting Camilla to develop delicacy, discretion, and other virtues. In numerous places he sermonizes like the clergyman that he is, although never from a pulpit. Dr. Marchmont, Edgar's mentor, provides additional sententious statements. Even the simple Sir Hugh chips in with several pages of advice, particularly when he believes that he is dying.

The result of all these discourses, along with Fanny's own pronouncements about matters, is that the didacticism overshadows and spoils the narrative effect. The textbook or courtesy book[15] qualities violate the illusion of reality by making readers aware that the author is controlling her characters according to her superimposed moral arguments instead of allowing the individuals to interact according to their nature and the situation. In her previous novels, Fanny's didacticism was more carefully camouflaged and was relieved by comic touches. In *Camilla* the satirical thrusts are so few and the humor is so slight that the high seriousness of the novel becomes overwhelming, especially in the last volumes.

Not everything in the novel is grim. Lionel, Camilla's brother, provides some levity as a boy with his innumerable practical jokes and pranks. However, like Sir Sedley Clarendal, a typical fop, Fanny transforms Lionel from a humorous individual to a serious one. He extorts money from his uncle, lavishes it on women, loses it by gambling, pleads with Camilla to give him more, and finally confesses that his lust for it has ruined his life. Sir Sedley changes from a fashionable fool early in the novel to an attractive suitor enamored of Camilla. Both these characters take on more humanlike attributes after Fanny ceases using them for comic effect and portrays them as individuals.

VII *Memorable Characters*

The most amusing and interesting person in the novel is Sir Hugh Tyrold, an amiable and lovable fool, reminiscent of Addison's Sir Roger, Fielding's Parson Adams, Smollett's Sir Launcelot Greaves, and Goldsmith's Dr. Primrose. Usually ridicule and derision play a large part in Fanny's comedy, but in creating Sir Hugh she displays the warmth and affection needed to reveal a character's absurdities without destroying his integrity. Thus the petty follies and weaknesses of Sir Hugh are more than counterbalanced by his benevolence, his humanity, his thoughtfulness, and his unselfishness. In contrast to the other characters, his candor about himself is refreshing. He discovers that he cannot learn Latin because he is "as sheer a blockhead as ever" and admits "there's some people can't learn." Nevertheless, he temporarily continues his studies out of courtesy and respect for the tutor whom he did not want to dismiss "merely for the fault of my having no head."

Even on his deathbed Sir Hugh remains in character despite the seriousness of the occasion. He asks his brother to preach the funeral sermon because "nobody else will speak of me so kindly; which may serve as a better lesson for those I leave behind." [16] The only regret that one has about Sir Hugh is that there is not enough of him in the novel. Others must have felt similarly because Mrs. Crewe wanted Fanny to continue his characterization later in a proposed periodical; the novelist declined to do so.

Next to Sir Hugh, the best delineated character is Mrs. Arlbery, conceived after Mrs. Thrale, Mrs. Montagu, and other women of wit and fashion. Like Mrs. Selwyn of *Evelina,* Mrs. Arlbery's sharp tongue spares neither the heroine nor others; and her masculine-like superiority makes her contemptuous of people. Fanny admires the nonconformity and aggressiveness of such women up to a point; however, she finds them unacceptable in the final analysis because the difference between the sexes should be maintained. Women should remain passive, submissive, patient, modest, delicate, and decorous. Consequently, Mrs. Arlbery's advice that Camilla should trifle with Sir Sedley proves harmful to the heroine, reflecting on the incompetence of the adviser.

Several other lesser characters occasionally are depicted well. Mrs. Mittin, a parasitic-like woman who attaches herself to Camilla, is a new type of individual, one not appearing previously in any of Fanny's works. The character's shrewdness and craftiness in outwitting the heroine are often cleverly depicted. Jacob, the groom, is one of Fanny's better lower-class people. His pungent dialogue filled with folk idioms, his ability to mimic his superiors, and his uninhibited and unrestrained comments add a refreshing note. Dr. Orkborne, the typical absent-minded pedant, sometimes provides a comic note as does Dubster the *nouveau riche* businessman; but both these characters are essentially stereotypes.

A few satirical scenes of balls are portrayed in Fanny's inimitable manner; several farcical episodes, such as those involving Lionel, are also well done. The best, an account of a country performance of *Othello* with ridiculous costumes, erroneous lines, absurd acting, and Othello's wig catching on fire is hilarious and rollicking, although like most farce, more effectively staged than described.

Yet these few fine scenes and well-delineated characters cannot save a novel burdened with melodrama and didacticism, overloaded with plot, and top-heavy with sentimental situations. Under the weight of these shortcomings, *Camilla* has sunk from public view.

CHAPTER 8

Playing at Playwriting

THE critics mixed faint praise with strong disapproval in reviewing *Camilla*. Although commending it as "a guide for the conduct of young females," they censured its stilted language, obtrusive didacticism, and inexcusable length.[1] Fanny rationalized their criticism by pointing out that in four months it had exceeded the sale of each of her former books by a third. She was willing to let her novels be judged by "the various multitude, not the fastidious few." [2]

She could well afford to ignore the disparaging remarks about *Camilla*. With the profit realized from its subscription and from the sale of the copyright to the publishers, Fanny and her husband leased land in Norbury Park, designed a home, hired workmen, and soon moved into what was to be known as Camilla Cottage. Fanny's letters and journals during this period concern her activities as proud mother, loving wife, and gracious hostess. Sitting freed from financial worries in her new cottage, listening to the innocent laughter of her young son, and basking in the bliss of married love, she naturally turned to romantic comedy.

I *What Should a Girl Do?*

Her first play written under these conditions obviously would uphold marriage based on love rather than on money, and enjoyed in rural rather than urban surroundings. In *Love and Fashion,* Fanny's heroine Hilaria has to choose between Love or Fashion—between marrying old, unattractive, wealthy Lord Ardville or handsome Valentine, whose "pitiful" six thousand pounds would make her "poor and obscure, and consequently miserable." Life with Lord Ardville in London promises to be exciting; with Valentine in the country it would be quiet. What should a girl do? Youth, love, and rural life are bound to triumph in romantic comedy, just as they had (excluding youth) in Fanny's life, and just as

they do in *Love and Fashion*. Those who would hope to have
the best of the two possible worlds—Love and Fashion—are de-
nied them. Valentine, Fanny's hero, points out that the two are
incompatible. True love, he declaims, blooms in the quiet of domestic life and dies in the constant public admiration that Fashion
requires.

The play reflects Fanny's personal convictions as much as it
does the conventions of romantic comedy. She could naturally in-
veigh against "the fashionable marriage based on appraisal of
equipage rather than character" and uphold "virtuous love . . as
truely the principle of conjugal happiness."[3] In addition, the
prosperous author could close her eyes to the rapidly increasing
taxes, recent poor harvests, and rigid social structure in exclaiming
rhetorically, "What is there of Fortune or distinction unattainable
in Britain by Talents, probity, and courage? . . . Has a man
hands, and shall he fear to work for the wife of his choice? Has a
woman a heart—and shall she barter her Person for Gold?"[4]

What mainly weakens *Love and Fashion* is Fanny's didacticism. Shakespeare's *As You Like It*,[5] which is similar in many respects, maintains a delicate balance between optimism and cyni-
cism, and between romance and irony. The Forest of Arden is a
fairyland inhabited by whimsical characters whose distresses are
not serious but comic. Fanny's country cottage, on the other hand,
is real. In addition, most of the play's humor stems from social satire, which assumes an actual world. The attempt to blend romantic comedy with comedy of manners was almost bound to fail
from the start. Despite these obstacles, Fanny almost brings it
off. However, her tendency to halt the action in order to lecture
the audience through her hero, Valentine, spoils the illusion of a
romantic never-never land and dulls the play by slackening its
swift pace and by detracting from its comical and amusing mood.

The first two acts are highly successful in setting forth Hilaria's
dilemma and in establishing the main characters. Lord Exbury,
impoverished by the extravagance of his son, Mordaunt, gives up
his residence in town; realizes that he cannot live with his inhos-
pitable brother, Lord Ardville; and moves to a country cottage.
Accompanying him are Mordaunt, his prodigal son; Valentine, his
model son; Miss Exbury, his socially aspiring daughter; Hilaria,
his beautiful ward; and Davis, his faithful servant. The main plot
deals with Hilaria's vacillating between marrying rich Lord Ard-

ville or poor Valentine. To enhance Valentine's cause, Fanny provides two country lovers, a woodcutter and haymaker (a version of Silvius and Phebe), who find happiness and contentment in each other. Swaying Hilaria in favor of Lord Ardville is her foppish cousin, Sir Archy Fineer, who vividly contrasts the dull uniformity of country life with the advantages that a fashionable marriage would bring: pin money, a title, a box at the opera, London life, and a widow's jointure.

The comic subplots involve Miss Exbury's schemes to win Sir Archy; Davis's efforts to attract Innis, Hilaria's maid; and Lord Exbury's attempts to cure Mordaunt of his extravagance. Although the situations are not particularly amusing, the "humour" characters provide some comedy. Davis, who speaks in hyperboles, is contrasted with Litchburn, an obsequious individual who comprehends only the literal meaning of words. Dawson, comedy's conventional braggart, believes that "there is not perhaps in the whole kingdom a Person that has a better temper than I have." [6] And Innis, the maid, fancies that every man, from her fellow servant Davis to the aristocratic Mordaunt, is secretly in love with her.

Fanny exhibits these individuals in amusing scenes. One of the most hilarious involves the inability of Lord Ardville to communicate with the literal-minded Litchburn. In others, Innis is entertainingly tricked into believing that different gentlemen love her; and Kate, the haymaker, comes to Mordaunt to fulfill a folk superstition requiring her to look at something frightful. In some places the lines are witty, especially Sir Archy's satirical description of a coquette.

At the play's end, Hilaria offers herself to Lord Ardville in order to save Valentine from going to jail for Mordaunt's debts. But, like Shakespeare's Duke Frederick and traditional comic villains, Ardville reforms. He steps aside to allow the lovers to marry, gives them a handsome gift, discharges Valentine's debts, and makes this young man his heir. In addition, Mordaunt repents, refusing to have Valentine arrested.

As if the main romantic plot, underplots, and cast of "humour" characters were not sufficient, Fanny, with her usual creative fertility, added something else—suspense and amusement furnished by a mysterious stranger and a ghost. The former turns out to be a bailiff looking for Valentine, while the latter is a dressmaker's dummy disguised in a dead woman's clothes to scare away lovers! It is almost as if Fanny is poking fun at the Gothic tendencies of the era, but her treatment is too straightforward in context to be ironic.

Mr. Harris, manager of the Covent Garden Theatre, saw possibilities in *Love and Fashion,* and probably realized the box-office appeal of Fanny's name. He suggested cutting down the long edifying speeches and eliminating some of the sentimental scenes. His offer of four hundred pounds for the manuscript must have made Fanny and her husband jubilant. Their joy was short-lived, however, because Dr. Burney objected violently to the staging of the play. Although he had not read *Love and Fashion,* he vividly remembered Fanny's embarrassing experience with *Edwy and Elgiva.* Like the dutiful and obedient daughter she was, Fanny withdrew her manuscript, but she wrote to her father with greater annoyance than ever expressed previously. At no other time except when she married, or was almost forced into marriage, did Fanny come so close to disregarding his advice.

II *Family Problems*

Something else—or rather several matters—"disencouraged" Fanny from trying to bring *Love and Fashion* to the boards. Most calamitous of these was the death of her closest and dearest sister, Susan. Living in Ireland with her family, Susan had persevered despite poor health, a philandering husband, uncomfortable living quarters, and the danger posed by Irish rebels and a French invasion. Finally, when she became seriously ill, her husband permitted Susan to travel to England. Charles and his son drove north to meet her while the other Burneys waited at home. They did so in vain because Susan died early in January, 1800, several days after Charles had found her gravely ill in her Parkgate lodgings.

For months Fanny could not recover from the loss of her beloved sister. The news of Susan's death—"that harrowing, never-to-be-forgotten moment of horror"—almost drove her out of her mind. Fanny remained sitting at home, brooding over this disaster and other misfortunes that had beset the family.

One of these had been the death of Mrs. Burney several years earlier. Although Fanny harbored no great affection for her stepmother, she realized Mrs. Burney's love and devotion to her husband, and Dr. Burney's dependence on her. After her loss, the family was disturbed by Charlotte's marriage to Ralph Broome. His Indian natural daughter and his Jacobean tendencies, plus his lack of personal charm, social grace, and sensitivity alienated the family. Fanny mentions this matter in her *Diary* but breathes no word about another affair, the closely held family secret about James and his half-sister, Sarah Harriet. Unhappy with his wife, Sally Payne, James left his home in September, 1798, to run away with Sarah. The Burneys told friends that James was separated from his wife and that Sarah was keeping house for him. Not until five years later was James happily reunited with Sally and his five children, and evidently forgiven by the Burneys.

No mention appears either in the published *Diary* of the marital problems of Maria Rishton, Fanny's stepsister, who finally deserted her Norfolk squire husband. Yet her difficulties must certainly have added to the cumulative grief occasioned by the loss of Susan, the death of Mrs. Burney with its attendant effect on Dr. Burney, the unfavorable marriage of Charlotte to Broome, and the unnatural living arrangement of James and Sarah.

Conditions outside the family circle were also depressing. There had been years of bad harvests, constant invasion threats from the French, a monetary crisis requiring a "loyalty loan" to help the war effort, an income tax, suspension of cash payments by the Bank of England, mutinies at Spithead and the Nore, ruthless and savage fighting in the Irish Civil War, the costly capitulation of the Duke of York's army after invading Holland, and hard repressive measures affecting civil liberties throughout England. Fanny mentions in passing many of these developments, but she fails to write about them at any length. Either she believed that as a woman she was unqualified to discuss them or else they were far removed from her tidy little life at West Hamble. Whatever the reason, she blocked family and national problems from her mind while completing two more comedies.

III *Another "Witlings"*

One of these, *The Woman Hater*, a revision of *The Witlings*, shows traces of influence from Molière, *Evelina*, and the comedy of intrigue. The leading character, Sir Roderick, might easily have been conceived by Molière. Jilted seventeen years before the play opens, when Miss Wilmot broke their engagement in order to marry Lord Smatter, Sir Roderick turned misogynist. Now elderly, he is fanatically committed to seeing that his heir also despises women. The leading candidate for his fortune, Jack Waverley, must agree to remain single. This young man, reared in Sir Roderick's country home in a monastic atmosphere, finds himself passionately attracted to all women; and he decides to torment the misogynist by marrying his former fiancée, now the widowed Lady Smatter. After an amusing visit with this wealthy woman, who constantly misquotes Pope, Swift, and Shakespeare, or else searches her mind in vain for a quotation (like her predecessor in *The Witlings*), Jack realizes the impossibility of living with her.

If the play had proceeded along these lines, all would have been well. However, Fanny introduced a complicated, sentimental subplot. Eleonora, Sir Roderick's sister, had deserted her jealous husband, Wilmot, because of his unwarranted cruelty. Separated for more than sixteen years, during which time Wilmot has learned of his wife's fidelity and his own error about her, they meet by coincidence upon returning to the village. Complications develop until Wilmot learns that Eleonora's daughter, Sophia, is actually his own, and that Joyce, whom he had brought up as his daughter, really is the nurse's child (similar to Sir John Belmont's situation in *Evelina*). Although such separations, accidental meetings, and instances of mistaken identity are the staple of comedy, they are used here for emotional effect. Eleonora, a forlorn, mysterious character (probably a revised Elberta, the heroine of Fanny's unfinished tragedy), belongs to the coterie of innocent, virtuous women who suffered throughout eighteenth-century literature. Her presence and plight detract from the play's humourous effect, although admirers of the popular sentimental comedies would not have objected.

Despite a weak subplot, *The Woman Hater* succeeds because Fanny allows her main comic characters to dominate most scenes. Sir Roderick vituperates and rants against the fair sex, particularly the educated ones. In his view, a woman should not be taught to read or write; she should know nothing except how "to sew a gown and make a Pudding." In particular he questions: "Must she study mathematics,—to count a Hen's nest? Must she understand Latin,—to stitch her Sampler? Must she pore over a Library, to find a Greek recipe for a Pudding?" [7] After berating the fair sex throughout the play with such fury and at such length, at the end he embraces Lady Smatter. This humorous reversal is effectively conceived.

Sir Roderick contains nearly all the attributes of a great comic figure. In the hands of Molière, he would have become an Alceste, not only a man with a comic incongruity but one with a justifiable obsession. Fanny, however, seldom allows us to laugh with Sir Roderick in his attacks against women. He is portrayed as an absurd stereotype instead of a disturbed human being. The author's own feministic views may have kept her from treating him with any kindness or understanding.

Yet she is not much gentler with her own sex. Lady Smatter is the same "humour" character that she was in Fanny's *Witlings*. However, in *The Woman Hater* she has a less important role, being offstage or downstage except for a scene or two. The de-emphasis of her part contributes to the comic effectiveness of this misquoting, pseudo-litterateur who suffered from overexposure in Fanny's first play.

Fanny's best conceived character is Joyce Wilmot, an uninhibited fun-loving young lady who acts like the model of propriety before her father but turns into a wildly dancing, singing hoyden behind his back. She is delighted to discover that she is not the daughter of Wilmot, who was always "ordering, and tutoring, and scolding, and managing . . . and reading!" Now she is free to be brash and candid. She chides Sir Roderick for saving his money when he has neither "child nor chick" to spend it on. If he would give her some, Joyce states, she would "go to plays, balls, operas, puppet shows, see all the wild beasts, eat all the tarts at the pastry cooks, and ride in a coach with brisk horses. . . ." [8] When this attack fails to yield her any money, she offers to love and kiss him, and to build "a large, huge, gigantic bonfire of all of Aunt Smatter's Books and Authors." Sir Roderick cannot resist this form of revenge. However, Joyce had already learned that Aunt Smatter's bookcases are filled not with fine things to read but with candy, cosmetics, and perfumes!

Far better suited to Joyce than wealthy Sir Roderick is Bob Sapling, a country bumpkin modeled after Bob Voluble in *The Witlings*. This illiterate oaf teams with the happy, carefree Joyce to provide a striking contrast to the frustrated, affectedly erudite Lady Smatter and the misogynistic Sir Roderick. At the end, it is

Joyce who reveals the truth about a woman-hater: "It is,—to hate a woman—if she won't let you love her—if you can't run to her; . . . and to vow she shall never cross your threshold,—unless she'll come to be mistress of your whole house!" [9]

The Woman Hater offers much to enjoy and laugh at but the discordant notes of the sentimental subplot spoil the humorous effect for present readers. Yet in Fanny's day, when laughter was mingled with tears, and sometimes with gasps of horror, the play might have been highly successful. No record is available of her interest in having it produced. She merely continued writing; but, unlike her novels which were progressively poorer, her plays improved. The next one, *A Busy Day*, stands as her best dramatic effort, and is worthy of being read and acted today along with such eighteenth-century favorites as Sheridan's *School for Scandal* and Goldsmith's *She Stoops to Conquer*.

IV *An Unpublished Masterpiece*

The heroine of *A Busy Day*, Eliza Watts, arrives in England from India, where she met and became secretly engaged to the hero, Cleveland. The play concerns the efforts of the lovers to overcome numerous misunderstandings and the opposition of his guardians. Just as the Delviles objected to Mortimer marrying Cecilia, so Sir Marmaduke and Lady Wilhelmina disapprove of Cleveland marrying a tradesman's daughter. To further complicate matters, Miss Percival has been selected as a desirable wife for Cleveland because she has generously loaned money to Sir Marmaduke, while Cleveland's younger brother, Frank, learning of Eliza's great wealth and ignorant of her secret engagement, decides to marry her.

This conventional comic plot dealing with the blocking efforts of others, particularly older people, to prevent young love from running smoothly, is supplemented by social satire in the tradition of the comedy of manners. As she did in *Evelina,* Fanny contrasts two classes in order to ridicule each, and embarrasses the heroine by having her middle-class relatives act boorishly and vulgarly before her fashionable friends. Cleveland is so shocked at Eliza's family that he asks in the stilted rhetoric of the day, "Sweet lovely Eliza! from weeds so coarse can a flower so fragrant bloom?" [10]

That Eliza is such a "flower" is evident in the following scene when Sir Marmaduke and Lady Wilhelmina, mistaking her for

Miss Percival's friend, are charmed by her refinement. Ironically, they contrast her with "that city-born girl" (the same Eliza) whom Frank has told them that he wishes to marry. As the younger son, he may select a wife socially beneath him, but Cleveland cannot marry Eliza. Or at least, not until the play's end when Sir Marmaduke, unable to borrow more money from Miss Percival to pay the mortgage, overlooks Eliza's "low" birth in view of her huge fortune.

In a closing speech pointing out that "Merit is limited to no spot and confined to no class," [11] Cleveland states far more democratic views than Fanny had allowed her characters to utter previously. Another reflection of her changed social thinking is that the middle-class characters come off far better than do the aristocrats. Sir Marmaduke and Lady Wilhelmina with their supercilious snobbery and blind intolerance are both obnoxious individuals, exaggerated into caricature, and at times so despicable that they become abominable rather than amusing. This same heavy touch was evident in *Evelina*, where Fanny lacerated the votaries of fashion at Mrs. Beaufort's for their heartless racing of the old women.

In *A Busy Day* Fanny continues to deride the aristocracy's cruelty by having Sir Marmaduke manifest indifference towards the villagers killed in a fire and by having Lady Wilhelmina contend that the loss of Lord German's hair is a greater blow than the breaking of her servant's legs. These callous views are supported by the actions of other members of the gentry—Miss Percival, Frank Cleveland, and Lord Dervis—who invite the Watts family to dinner, and then rudely ignore them. While the result is amusing because the guests deserve little sympathy, Fanny leaves no question about the vulgarity of the aristocracy, although some doubt exists about their credibility.

Far more acceptable as realistic characters, although not so savagely derided, are Eliza's mother and sister, conceived in the tradition of the Branghtons. From the moment they arrive at the dinner party finding fault with Mr. Watts, to their affectations at its end, they are constantly squabbling among themselves, acting obsequiously to their betters, revealing their ignorance of social customs, and pretending to forget their humble past. Both mother and daughter are made memorable by numerous gems of dialogue, such as Mrs. Watts's attempt to impress others with her

coach and servants by stating: "I dare say Robert's forgot to tell
Thomas to order Richard to stop." [12]

Previously Fanny had satirized the gentry and the parvenus;
never before had she attempted to cope sympathetically with the
ironic plight of members of the upper middle class with the
money but not the manners to mingle in polite society. Two characters, Watts and Tibbs, who are concerned with this problem,
add a new dimension to the play. Although both are comic characters, they are bathed in the gentle light of satire rather than its
harsh glare. Watts, now a successful, retired businessman, unhappy with his present leisure, misses the activity and respect to
which he was formerly accustomed, realizes that he is disliked by
his fashionable acquaintances, hates having his wig dressed daily
and discarding new clothes for newer ones, and worries about the
increasing demands for money from his wife and eldest daughter.
One can both laugh at and sympathize with Watts. Lacking the
affectations of the other comic characters, he is honest about himself and thereby appealing in his simple, unsophisticated way. Innocent of malice and ignorant of manners, he is both pitiful and
amusing, but praiseworthy for not having become crudely ambi-
tious like his wife or vulgarly selfish like his eldest daughter.
There is in the characterization of Watts much of the wholesome
humor that Fanny had used to depict her most appealing comic
character, Sir Hugh Tyrold in *Camilla*.

Tibbs, who knew Watts as an errand boy and his wife as a
house maid, adds both satire and sanity to the play. Still impoverished, he fails to understand why his wealthy friend is not enjoying his fine house, coach, and servants. Like Captain Mirvan in
Evelina, Tibbs has no social pretensions and often speaks with
common sense in a world devoid of normality. When Watts
complains of being ill-treated by the gentry, Tibbs tells him
bluntly, "Why then don't take off your hat to them; & don't get off
your chair to them; & don't answer them when they speak to
you." [13] As for Watts's complaints about his wife and eldest daughter, Tibbs advises him to "mind them no more than a cat." In the
closing scene, when he and Watts are ignored by the aristocrats at
the dinner party, Tibbs repays the gentry in kind by stretching
out on a sofa.

The presence of Tibbs and Watts and the absence of Fanny's
intrusive didacticism and distracting sentimentality carry the play

to heights she had never before attained. *A Busy Day* is also helped by several farcical devices. There is the mistaken identity of the two Watts daughters (Eliza and Peg), and of Lord Dervis's valet for the lord himself. There is also much stage business about the ludicrous wigs worn by Watts and Tibbs, Mrs. Watts's new shoes, her inability to read a letter, and her pretense not to recognize Tibbs at a party and, in turn, his unwillingness to forget how she scrubbed floors as a maid. The play is further enhanced by Fanny's inimitable use of idiomatic dialogue. Particularly amusing are Tibbs's "Fegs!", Lord Dervis's "O the Deuce!", and Peg's "La, Pa!"

The weaknesses marring Fanny's other comedies are not present in *A Busy Day*. The absence of obtrusive comments has been mentioned, but also noteworthy is the omission of a subplot, which usually contained a sentimental story that detracted from the comic mood and was also poorly integrated into the main plot. The tightly unified *Busy Day* centers about the love problems of Eliza and Cleveland, moving swiftly from one amusing predicament to another with little reliance on chance or coincidence, and no time or provocation for tears or sighs. In addition to the lack of didacticism and sentimentality, the play deals with the world that Fanny knew best and had depicted successfully before.

In portraying satirically the clash between different social groups with their respective manners and codes, Fanny returned to the formula that had made *Evelina* so successful. Although her hero is still stiff and wooden, and her upper class figures continue to be cruelly exaggerated, she had broadened her range of characters to include servants (the talkative Deborah and the polished butler) and such individuals as Watts and Tibbs, who are humorously portrayed without being strongly satirized. Fanny, who has also learned how to improve the pace of a play, handles the opening scene of Eliza's arrival deftly by introducing most of the characters, establishing some of the complications, and then proceeding from this point to add other characters and complications without lingering too long on one situation or overexposing any of her comic crew. Everything moves with swiftness and verve to the hilarious grand finale, the dinner party where the contrasting social groups are devastatingly depicted.

Despite an intervening century and a half, *A Busy Day* continues to possess an appealing freshness and sparkle found in few other eighteenth-century comedies. It was the work that Dr. Johnson, Mrs. Thrale, Sheridan, and others hoped that Fanny would write. She finally did but about twenty-two years after the ill-fated *Witlings*. Unfortunately, neither *Love and Fashion,* which would have pleased the sentimental taste of the period, nor *A Busy Day* was ever produced. If they had been, Fanny might have commenced a new career as a dramatist, and would have been better known and recognized today. Instead, the manuscripts were put aside because she was soon on her way to France.

CHAPTER 9

A Wandering Author

AFTER several unsuccessful attempts to obtain his pension, General d'Arblay was promised it providing he served in St. Domingo with General Le Clerc. Learning of this offer, Fanny implored her husband "to weigh, weigh . . . in the *detail*" anything that would require his giving up his "*time, leisure, hours, gardening, scribbling,* and *reading.*" [1] But she failed to realize his concern about a matter that he had mentioned previously: "Il est impossible de nous dissumuler que depuis plusieurs années nous n'avons vécu, malgré toute notre économie, que par le moyen de resources qui sont ou epuisees ou bien prêtes à l'être" ("It is impossible to deceive ourselves of the fact that for several years we have lived, despite all our economizing, only by means of resources that are either exhausted or about to be").[2] Anxious to obtain his pension, d'Arblay agreed to serve but only on the condition that he would not be required to fight later against the English. Not until after he had arrived in Paris did he learn that Napoleon was unwilling to accept him under these terms, despite the pleas of Lafayette.

Stranded due to passport restrictions, d'Arblay asked Fanny to join him with Alex. Although apprehensive about traveling alone and leaving her seventy-six-year-old father, Fanny hastened to her husband. The account of her trip and the following years in France consists of charming vignettes or exciting adventures often written long after they had occurred. Yet they are so vividly related that Fanny conveys the feeling of immediacy without the reader's being aware of the time gap. The emphasis, as formerly, is on people and incidents rather than descriptions of the countryside or personal revelations.

Her account of the coach trip to Dover, for example, mentions neither her queasiness about leaving home for a foreign country nor her reactions to the spring scenes along the route. Instead, she

117

deals with the interplay among the passengers, many of whom might have appeared in her novels. They include the haughty, pompous Monsieur Anglais, who hastily grabbed the best seat for himself—"a gentleman born, though not gently bred"; Mme Raymond, a French "gentlewoman" with a horror of having anyone come near her bulging petticoats because, as she later revealed, they concealed some lace that she was smuggling through customs; and Mme Blaizeau, "a gay, voluble, good-humoured, and marry [sic] woman," who entertained the group with intimate accounts of her courtship by a gentleman farmer and her experiences as governess to some young English ladies.

I *Life and People—French Style*

In Paris, Fanny describes the touching reunion with her husband and the interesting meetings with numerous *ci-devants*. These former members of the nobility impressed her with their stories of suffering during the Revolution. She was moved by the stark contrast between their former elegance and their present proud but sparse existence. Fanny, always sympathetic, is touched by the pitiable plight of those fallen from their aristocratic life; but she never probes into or speculates about their former unjust or oppressive ways. Whatever egalitarian ideas she may have had extended only to middle-class women and not to the lower classes. Like most English writers of the period, she seems unaware of their existence or their problems; consequently, one would hardly expect her to indicate any social concern for the French masses.

Under such conditions Fanny was favorably impressed with everyone whom she met and with everything that she saw in Paris. She was greatly honored by Mme de Lafayette, who climbed three flights of stairs, despite her lameness, to call upon Fanny. Former acquaintances and friends of her husband, such as Princesse d'Henin, Mme de Maisonneuve, and Princesse de Poix, escorted her to assemblies and accompanied her to the Italian opera. Everywhere she found people to be highly cultured and charming with a fine sense of propriety, courtesy, and decorum.

Most memorable of Fanny's experiences in Paris was attending a parade at the Tuileries to watch Napoleon review his troops, and to observe him before and afterwards. As if aware that her reactions would be read and repeated widely in England, she changed from her customary informal style to a swollen rhetoric saturated with quoted phrases. Although stating that Napoleon looked exactly like the busts and medallions of him that she had seen, Fanny was surprised at his demeanor. He appeared like "a profoundly studious and contemplative man, who 'o'er books consumes' not only the 'midnight oil' but his own daily strength, and 'wastes the puny body to decay' by abstruse speculation and theoretic plans or rather visions, ingenious but not practicable." He looked like anything but the bold, daring, intrepid commander who had proven to be invincible in battle. His air of "melancholy and meditation," his plain dress that contrasted conspicuously with the dazzling finery around him, and his "countenance, so 'sicklied o'er with the pale hue of thought,'" suggested the cloistered student rather than the hardy soldier.[3]

Several months later her husband purchased an inexpensive house at Passy, two miles outside of Paris. By that time d'Arblay had finally been granted his retirement pension, although it amounted to only half of what he had expected. To supplement the meager amount, he obtained a clerical position in the Ministry of the Interior. Despite his lengthy day, the perfunctory nature of his work, and his inability to regain any of his inherited property worth about twenty thousand dollars, D'Arblay and Fanny lived contentedly in "enviable retirement." Their house was "unfurnished . . . unpapered, and every way unfinished"; but the view of Paris and the surrounding country was magnificent; and life was peaceful and pleasant.

Outside the world was not so serene. Continuing friction between Napoleon and the English resulted in the resumption of fighting in May, 1803. Aware that getting letters to her father would be difficult, Fanny hastened to send him word of her distress at the war news, and to include a prayer "to bless and preserve my beloved father, and to restore the nations to peace, and me to his arms."[4]

For the next nine years, Fanny's correspondence was sparse. Many letters were undoubtedly lost as communication with England became increasingly difficult. In addition, she had little incentive to write frequently, knowing that her letters were not being received. Nor did she keep her journal regularly. Most of what she wrote reveals disappointment at not hearing from the members of her family, her friends, and her aging father. In 1810 she proudly informed Dr. Burney that he had been elected to the

Beaux Arts Classe of the Institute of France. Other letters describe Alex winning awards at school, visits with friends, a return move to Paris because of d'Arblay's arduous and fatiguing walk to and from work in winter, and the bliss occasioned by the arrival of a rare message from England. The tone of her letters is somber and sad; her flashes of playfulness are rare. Words like "dreams" and "prayers" recur. The long absence from her father, family, and friends was mentally depressing and physically wearing.

In 1811 her health took a turn for the worse from another cause —a metastic abscess, probably a cancer, which finally necessitated an operation. Unfortunately, her graphic account of this torturous episode and the entire illness is omitted from the published *Diary*.[5] Fanny evidently did not wish to disclose her embarrassment about disrobing or to describe the frank physical details of the operation. When the manuscript account is printed with her complete works, it will stand as another testimonial to her skill as a writer and to her fortitude as a person.

She tells the story well, setting the crude bedroom scene in detail with its compresses, sponges, two old mattresses, and a sheet. The team of seven black-robed men arrive, led by M. Dubois and Baron de Larrey, surgeons to Empress Josephine and Napoleon, respectively. At that date, because anesthetics were rarely used, Fanny was conscious during the operation. She describes people bending over her, the glitter of polished steel, the tracing of a cross and a circle on her breast, the excruciating incision, the agonizing pain, her own screaming, and even a consultation in which M. Dubois insisted that some additional cutting and scraping were necessary. Finally it was over, only to be followed by a long night of suffering. Soon the pain eased and Fanny slowly recovered, weakened by the experience but strong enough to lead an active life for many years to come. For her courage during the operation, and her devising a plan to keep her husband away to spare him her suffering, she was named "l'Ange."

II *Home Again*

After completely recuperating, Fanny renewed her efforts to return to England. Finally in 1812, when Alex was on the verge of being drafted into the French army to fight against his countrymen, she obtained passports for America and booked passage for

herself and her son on an American vessel clandestinely stopping
at Dover. After several harrowing experiences Fanny and Alex
landed at Deal where she celebrated her joy by picking up a
bright pebble and pressing it to her lips.

The long awaited reunion with her father took place shortly
afterwards in Chelsea. They met alone in the library. Although
pretending to be "gay and cheering," Fanny was saddened by his
physical deterioration. The former vigorous, vivacious man of sev-
enty-six was now a feeble recluse of eighty-six. He was "weak,
weak, and changed—his head almost always hanging down, and
his hearing most cruelly impaired." [6]

During the ten-year period Fanny had also changed, as had her
financial resources. Money was now acutely needed for Alex's education and living expenses. Turning once again to her "scribbling," she completed *The Wanderer*, begun in France. When it
appeared in 1814, Fanny received about five hundred pounds
(ten thousand dollars) despite unfavorable reviews,[7] the novel's
high price (about forty dollars), and some misunderstanding
about her contract with Longman and Rees, the publishers. *The
Wanderer* added to her low financial resources but detracted from
her high literary reputation.

III   *The Last Novel*

Although the plot of *The Wanderer* follows Fanny's staple formula—a woman suffers countless distresses until united with the
man whom she loves—the novel is similar to her first three in
few other respects. Instead, it is a story of suspense and intrigue
with borrowings from the Gothic novel, the novel of social theory,
and the picaresque. Hardly evident is any comedy or high-spirited
farce. The delightfully amusing touches that had illuminated *Evelina*, much of *Cecilia*, and some of *Camilla* are almost totally missing. Rather than continue in her previous comic vein, Fanny, writing in the tradition of her own tragedies, imitated the popular
novels of the day without deviating from her concern with women
—their place, their problems, and the necessity of their acting
with propriety and acquiring prudence.

Although lacking the supernatural and chivalric elements typi-
fying the Gothic Romance, *The Wanderer* maintains much of its
atmosphere of horror, terror, and mystery. The novel opens on
this note with a magnificent, sonorous, periodic sentence: "During

the dire reign of the terrific Robespierre and in the dark of night, braving the cold, the darkness and the damps of December, some English passengers, in a small vessel, were preparing to glide silently from the coast of France, when a voice of keen distress resounded from the shore, imploring, in the French language, pity and admission." [8]

Despite the stranger's dirty appearance, soiled clothes, and the loss of her purse, the ship's occupants take her aboard and provide for her at an inn after landing in England; but they fail to learn her name or her history because she has vowed not to disclose any information. As the novel continues, clues about the heroine's past are gradually revealed during critical scenes with numerous libertines, heartless women, and a few benevolent souls. After having endured humiliation and ridicule as a companion and music teacher; failure and cruelty as a milliner, mantua-maker, and shop-owner; and terror and horror as a helpless stranger fleeing from unknown villainous pursuers, the heroine is finally seized by a man identified as her French husband, who in turn is shortly arrested by the police.

At this point she reveals that she is Juliet Granville, unknown daughter of the dead Lord Granville by his secret first marriage to a commoner. Like Evelina, Juliet was brought up by a man not related to her, a kindly bishop who had been legally assured of a legacy for her on condition that she marry and remain in France. A malevolent emissary from Robespierre, learning of these provisions, forced Juliet to wed him by threatening to kill the imprisoned bishop. But, before consummating the marriage and signing the legal document transferring the legacy to her husband, Juliet escaped, fled to England, and remained incognito to protect both herself and the bishop. On several occasions she was almost reluctantly compelled to reveal her identity, particularly once when her half-brother, acting on misinformation, attempted to rape her; but each time she was able to avoid the predicament without disclosing her secret. With her husband jailed, she is finally able to account for her strange actions.

Fanny drags the novel out as Juliet undergoes the humiliation of being accused as a thief. Then she hears that her husband, released from jail and sent to France, has seized the bishop and threatens to execute him unless Juliet returns. As fortune and Fanny have it, just as Juliet is about to board a boat, the bishop himself arrives with word that her husband is dead and that their marriage was not legal. Now a free and happy woman, Juliet can wed the faithful Harleigh, who has helped her, watched over her, and suffered with her, despite her statements that she could never marry him.

The melodramatic plot might have furnished the basis for an exciting novel, but the work is spoiled mainly by Fanny's failure to handle the point of view effectively and to avoid moralizing extensively. If the story had been told for its own sake—to entertain the reader and allow him to experience the plight of the heroine—and if Fanny had been more concerned with the technique of telling it, *The Wanderer* would at least have been enjoyable. Instead, a dull, disjointed book, it is mainly of historical and biographical interest.

IV Faulty Technique

In her previous novels, Fanny projected the story mainly through her heroines' minds. Most of *Evelina* is told in the heroine's candid letters, and *Cecilia* and *Camilla* are related by an omniscient author, mainly from the point of view of their heroines. In all these novels, readers are fully aware of why these women act as they do; nothing about them is withheld. In *The Wanderer*, Fanny also projects most of the story through her heroine's mind, but she unnaturally restricts Juliet's thoughts to the present and future, never allowing her to reflect on the past because to do so would reveal who she is and what has happened to her. This artificial limitation results in numerous ridiculous and false situations that become especially apparent when Juliet discloses her identity at the novel's end. For example, although meeting and befriending her half-sister and brother, Lord Melbury and Lady Aurora, she never for a moment thinks about their relationship, the coincidence of meeting them, or the incestuous horror of his attempting to rape her!

In two other places, Fanny's artistic ineptness with her means of telling most of the story through Juliet's mind is particularly disconcerting. About midway in the novel, Juliet learns that her childhood friend Gabriella is in England. Frantically Juliet searches for her, finally finding her. The scene of their reunion, therefore, is climactic, but after momentarily showing their joyous reconciliation, Fanny crudely draws the curtain so that their lengthy conversation about the past will be withheld. Fanny was determined to maintain suspense at any price. For the same reason, when Juliet's mysterious husband suddenly appears and whisks her into his room, readers are jerked from viewing the scene through her terror-stricken mind to watching it through Harleigh's perplexed one. This abrupt switch in the middle of this violent episode preserves the mystery of the heroine's past but provokes the reader.

As a result of these technical blemishes, verisimilitude, so necessary in such a melodramatic story, is violated because the author, in arbitrarily withholding information and controlling the action, is too clearly evident. Fanny would have been far wiser to have revealed Juliet's secret to readers and allowed them to share her anguish, distress, and frustration. The dramatic irony resulting from this approach in such scenes as those cited involving Juliet and her half-brother and sister would have more than compensated for the loss in suspense.

V *Tedious Teaching*

Also detracting from *The Wanderer's* effectiveness are its numerous didactic passages. In her previous novels, Fanny was mainly concerned with stressing the importance of prudence to innocent, inexperienced, virtuous women. She also spoke out against dueling, gambling, lack of benevolence, a classical education for women, and some social evils of the day. In *The Wanderer* she turns her attention to theological, political, and philosophical problems with disastrous results. Most of these issues are introduced in connection with Elinor Joddrell's ardent love for Harleigh, and her eternal and endless questioning of him about evil, atheism, afterlife, and suicide. Although Elinor raises these problems, and serves as a love foil, she plays an unnecessary role in the novel. She appears in numerous lengthy scenes but mainly to raise these issues and to create the Gothic atmosphere with her wild rantings and ravings and with her dramatic suicide attempts. Sometimes these are so melodramatic as to be ludicrous: for example, in her second suicide effort, Elinor, disguised as a masked man, plunges a dagger into her breast before a large audience during Juliet's public concert. The scene is flooded with bathos: "The blood gushed out in torrents, while, with a smile of triumph and eyes of idolizing love, she dropt into his [Harleigh's] arms, and clinging round him, feebly articulated, 'Here let me end!—accept the oblation—and the just tribute—of these dear, delicious last moments!' " [9] Elinor's third attempt, in a cemetery by a tombstone bearing her name, ends grotesquely with her believing that she is actually dead though the effort has been thwarted.

Elinor Joddrell can best be understood as a feminine counterpart of Goethe's Werther. Numerous novels written by women, such as Mary Wollstonecraft's *Mary, a Fiction* and Mme de Stael's *Corinne* were declaring a new freedom for women, equality between the sexes, and greater political and religious liberty. These passionate, romantic "new" heroines, who led independent and unconventional lives in these novels, were far too masculine for Fanny. She was interested in the economic and social plight of women but she was appalled at any suggestion that they be as free from restraints as men. Therefore, Elinor, a feminine rebel, serves as an example of what happens to such a woman. She loses Harleigh, her convictions, and almost her mind. In the end, she had learned from him in innumerable lectures (one lasts about thirty pages) that there is a life hereafter, suicide is morally wrong, the soul exists, and religion should be accepted on faith. Elsewhere, for the further edification of readers, Fanny disparages revolutionary political principles, new rights for women, and changes in the social system.

The emphasis on repudiating Elinor and progressive ideas detracts from an otherwise well-unified plot. In *Camilla,* Fanny inserted huge didactic sections to educate her readers and to justify her work in terms of its moral value. Although the length of this material was objectionable, it was at least well integrated into the novel. In *The Wanderer,* Fanny's instructional passages are far more numerous without being closely related to the plot. Where previously the didacticism spoiled her work, here it ruins it.

Closely allied in theme with the discrediting of Elinor's romantic views is the disparagement of rural existence. Rousseau-inspired concepts about country bliss, the peace and contentment of village life, and the purity, honesty, and happiness of hardworking men and women are sharply punctured. When Juliet flees from her pursuers, she meets harvest-men, market-women, peddlers, ballad-singers, farmers, village girls, and workmen in the New Forest. Although treated kindly by some, Juliet mainly experiences rudeness, hostility, and lack of sympathy.

In addition, the poor are not all engaged in productive, honest toil. While wandering in a dark cottage, Juliet discovers blood on her hand and then notes sacks apparently filled with bodies. This Gothic scene ends when the people living there are revealed to be deer poachers rather than murderers. In a later episode, Juliet is at first impressed with the apparent happiness and cheerfulness of a farmer's family. After staying with them, she soon perceives their empty, dull lives, their helplessness before natural forces affecting crops, their long hours of drudgery, and their blindness to the beauty surrounding them. She also notes that women are treated like menial servants because they fail to earn money by working in the fields. Consequently, the joy and happiness of those living close to nature are only an illusion.

VI   *Echoes of the Picaresque*

This section of the novel devoted to Juliet's adventures in the New Forest presents a panorama of country life and people. Like other parts of *The Wanderer,* it is indebted to the picaresque tradition. Obviously Fanny's novel does not involve a picaresque hero, usually a good-natured rascal used as a lens through which readers can view society; but Smollett's statement in his preface to *Roderick Random* applies almost equally as well to her novel: "I have attempted to represent modest merit struggling with every difficulty to which a friendless orphan is exposed, from his own want of experience, as well as from the selfishness, envy, malice, and base indifference of mankind."

In similar fashion, Juliet, a penniless woman without friends or family to protect her, tries to exist in a cruel, heartless society. Her attempt to find refuge among the country people has been described; in two other sections of the novel she seeks friendship and employment among fashionable society, and then among tradespeople. Her efforts to do needlework, to give harpsichord lessons, and to serve as a companion are all made impossible and unpalatable by the malice, intolerance, selfishness, and viciousness of her upper-class employers, patrons, and pupils. Fanny depicts the heartless Mrs. Maple, the sarcastic Mrs. Ireton, the tyrannical Mrs. Howel, and the snobbish Mrs. Arbe so mercilessly that they are hardly credible.

Just as these women persecute Juliet, so she is similarly mistreated by customers, employers, and fellow employees when she operates a business with Gabriella, serves as a seamstress in a millinery shop, and becomes a mantua-maker. Juliet also receives an education in the slow-down practices imposed by piece-goods employees, the unethical tricks of shopowners, and the immorality of working girls. In general, *The Wanderer,* an episodic chronicle of the adventures and experiences of a penniless, single woman, presents a mordant exposé of upper, middle, and lower classes in various occupations and in rural and urban surroundings.

The structure of the novel allowed Fanny to deal with a subject always close to her heart: the plight of the single, unprovided woman. The subtitle of the novel, *Female Difficulties,* indicates Fanny's interest in the problems confronting an accomplished, educated, well-bred woman without financial support. Juliet tries one means after another to earn a living but all without success. Fanny ends on an optimistic note by stating that Juliet's problems are not insurmountable as long as "mental courage, operating through patience, prudence, and principle, supply physical force, combat disappointment, and keep the untamed spirits superior to failure, and ever alive to hope." [10] Yet few readers will accept such a conclusion in view of Juliet's experiences. Her happiness results from her birthright, not from her indomitable will. The hardships of such women could not merely be wished away in this manner.

Fanny's close identification with the economic plight of her heroine may have prevented her from writing in a light, amusing manner. Just as the world is tragic to the man who feels and comic to the one who thinks, so Fanny's concern for Juliet may have been responsible for the absence of her typical scenes of farce or social satire. When she occasionally ridicules individuals, such as the society matrons—Mrs. Maple, Mrs. Ireton, and Mrs. Howel— she does so in the heavy style of Juvenal rather than with her usual Horatian wit. Yet there are some exceptions: Tedman, a prosperous grocer, criticizes his daughter but is pleased that she wishes to take music lessons to become socially acceptable. Fanny allows readers to laugh pleasantly at his gaucheness but to respect him for being the only person to pay Juliet.

Three other amusing characters are Giles Arbe, a comically absent-minded, benevolent simpleton who is generous to a fault; Sir Jasper Herrington, a superannuated beau, who concocts fanciful

tales about communicating with elves, fairies, and imps; and the
Admiral, an English salt like Captain Mirvan, who occasionally
expresses his chauvinistic views in colorful nautical language
which almost allows one to excuse the absurd coincidence of his
turning out to be Juliet's maternal uncle. In a few places, some of
the lower-class characters, such as Gooch, Stubbs, and Scope, provide humor, especially with their inane questions about France
and "Robert Spierre."

Although Fanny exhibits relatively little of her talent for comedy, she does display superb ability in presenting scenes and characters dramatically. The opening chapters of her other novels
were expository. In *The Wanderer* no authorial explanatory statements occur from the opening sentence until the beginning of the
fourth chapter. During this time the numerous passengers aboard
the boat are clearly characterized by their reactions to the stranger taken aboard. It is a masterful display of the superb artistry
that Fanny only occasionally demonstrated in her later years.

Also skillfully executed are several scenes in which landscape
plays an effective role in creating atmosphere. Usually Fanny ignores the settings, but here, particularly in the cemetery episode
with Elinor and in a New Forest scene when a fierce dog terrifies
Juliet, the landscape contributes effectively to the mood. Elsewhere, in descriptions of Stonehenge, a sunset, and the sea, Fanny
reveals a surprising Romantic tendency to view Nature as an ema-
nation of God.

VII   *A Summation*

In a final analysis of *The Wanderer,* however, one must admit
that Fanny's moments of artistry are too few and far between.
The bulk of the novel is concerned with Juliet Granville, a feminine paragon who prevails over almost every conceivable distress
and humiliation. Because her difficulties result from the unbelievable viciousness of others rather than from her own innocence or
weakness, because of her irreproachable perfection, and because
of her restricted mind that reflects only on the present and not on
the past, Juliet is neither interesting nor credible. Sometimes her
concern for propriety causes her to make ridiculous decisions
when choosing between violating punctilio or taking dangerous
risks. One such instance results in her exposing herself to the

possibility of being seized by her husband rather than remaining in the safety of Harleigh's room.

Just as Juliet is not believable, neither is Harleigh. One questions his eternal devotion to the heroine despite her unequivocal rejection of him and her unknown social status. Also incredible is his patience in explaining to Elinor in frequent interminable lectures why she should not commit suicide but should believe in God. Harleigh talks in the stilted rhetoric of Lord Orville, Mortimer Delvile, and Edgar Mandlebart; and, like them, he is ubiquitous, appearing often at highly improbable moments to Juliet's great embarrassment or relief.

Most obvious of the novel's many weaknesses are Fanny's ponderous and laborious style, which had evidently become even more artificial and stilted from her sojourn in France, and her dependence upon coincidence, particularly in having each of the boat's passengers reappear later to play an important role. There is no doubt but that *The Wanderer* is Fanny's poorest novel. Its weakness may stem from trying to write not what she could do best but what she felt would sell best. Unfortunately, the work is a far cry from the simple story of *Evelina* that had won her renown.

The first novel's wry picture of peaceful and quiet London drawing rooms is replaced by the excitement and suspense of an adventure story involving spies, smugglers, suicide attempts, and an extended chase. Melodramatic and romantic rantings take the place of the sly remark, the embarrassed blush, and the obsequious compliment. Massive doses of didacticism supplant occasionally edifying statements. Callous and cruel characters dominate pages where formerly vain and self-centered people had bowed and strutted. A heavy, sluggish style is substituted for a fresh, natural, sprightly one. Gone are the comic touches, the realistic dialogue, the memorable characterizations. Without an editor, without a competent critic to guide her, and without the ability to realize her own limitations, Fanny ventured out of the range of her genius. The result, a disappointment in its own day to her friends and followers, is read today only by Burneyites and dedicated scholars of the eighteenth-century novel.

CHAPTER 10

Exciting Adventures and Disappointing Memoirs

ABOUT a month after the publication of *The Wanderer*, the eighty-eight-year-old Dr. Burney died. Although Fanny realized that "his sufferings had far surpassed his enjoyments" in recent months, she was deeply distressed. She recalled but could not heed her father's wise advice: "sorrow . . . requires time, as well as wisdom and religion, to digest itself; and till that time is both accorded and well employed, the sense of its uselessness serves but to augment, not mitigate, its severity." [1]

Dr. Burney may have conveyed this sentiment to his daughter but he undoubtedly expressed it clearer. Such turgid, obfuscating sentences, however, abound in Fanny's later writings, even in her *Diary*. Noticeable are the abundance of latinated words, the piling up of clause upon clause, the frequent sententious comments, and the greater use of personification and periphrasis. In the last volume of the *Diary*, Fanny's frequent recourse to her grand style may be attributed to her writing formally to posterity instead of informally to her father, family, and friends.

Nevertheless, her account of meeting Louis XVIII, of retreating from Paris to Brussels, of being terrified and confused during Waterloo, of traveling five days alone to the injured d'Arblay at Trier, and of finding herself trapped in a cave with rising water during a storm are among the most memorable incidents in the *Diary*. What compensates in part for her ponderous style is greater use of visual detail and more concern with mood and atmosphere, particularly in presenting panoramic scenes in vivid descriptive passages.

In writing some eleven years later about her meeting with Louis XVIII in London, Fanny reconstructs the details so effectively that the reader is unaware of the intervening time lapse. She may have embellished the episode by stressing her trepidation and diffidence, and by enlarging upon the King's praise of her, her novels, and her husband. But the description of her reactions is consistent with Fanny's characterization throughout the *Diary,* and Louis XVIII may well have been numbered among her many French admirers. Contributing to the effectiveness of her account, in addition to the delightful character sketches of the brash Irish heiress and other individuals, is the depiction of the confusion and excitement created by the milling crowd of English and French nobility. Fanny achieved a dimension seldom found elsewhere in the *Diary* by conveying graphically the festive, excited atmosphere of the occasion.

I   *From Paris to Waterloo*

The story of Fanny's flight from Paris during Napoleon's Hundred Days also captures vividly the mood prevalent at the time despite lapses into the intrusive grand style. In February, 1815, Fanny was living in Paris with her husband, a member of the King's special bodyguard. When Napoleon was welcomed in Lyons, the Parisians panicked. Fanny was too concerned with writing eloquently to describe the transformation visually: "Expectation was then awakened—consternation began to spread; and report went rapidly to her usual work, of now exciting nameless terror, and now allaying even reasonable apprehension." [2] Public anxiety subsided as Marshal Ney departed with his men to halt Napoleon, promising to bring Bonaparte to Paris in an iron cage. Louis XVIII proclaimed that he would never abandon his throne or leave the capital.

But the calm was short-lived. The next day Fanny noted that "all hope disappeared." In her grand style she continued: "From north, from south, from east, from west, alarm took the field, danger flashed its lightnings, and contention growled its thunders." [3] What caused the change is not stated; Fanny probably could not bear to mention Ney's defection with his troops upon seeing Napoleon.

At this time D'Arblay received his battle orders. Fanny describes their dramatic parting with restraint, simplicity, and sensitivity. Her rhetorical excesses are forgotten; she treats the emotionally charged incident with less sentimentality and more poignancy than she had displayed in her novels. In simple words she recounts how they prayed together and then separated. At the door, d'Arblay turned back, "and with a smile which, though forced, had inexpressible sweetness, he half-gaily exclaimed, 'Vive le Roi!'" Fanny, realizing that he desired to leave with "apparent cheerfulness," echoed his words. Then he departed from her sight. Wishing to see him again, she rushed to the window only to watch him "armed and encircled with instruments of death—bayonets, lances, pistols, guns, sabres, daggers!—what horror assailed me at the sight!" In minutes he rode away. Fanny suggests the contrast between the tormenting anguish within her and the silence without: "The street was empty; the gay constant gala of a Parisian Sunday was changed into fearful solitude: no sound was heard but that of here and there some hurried footstep. . . ." [4]

Fanny herself prepared to flee. While she was getting her things together and saying goodbye to friends, a dramatic note arrived from her husband: "Ma chère ami—tout est perdu! Je ne puis entrer dans aucun détail—de grâce, partez! le plutôt sera le mieux. A la vie et à mort, A d'A." ("My dear friend—all is lost! I cannot go into any detail—I beg of you, leave! The sooner the better. In life and in death. A d'A.").[5] Hastily Fanny left to accompany Princesse d'Henin and Comte de Lally-Tollendal in their flight to Brussels. They drove hurriedly over rough roads, fearful of pursuit and capture, stopping only at nearly empty inns and small "hovels" where tenants of Princesse d'Henin resided. There were interminable delays waiting for prefects to examine passports and to approve passage through towns.

Once Fanny had to pose as the *première femme de chambre* in order to conceal her identity as the wife of a general. The sensitive Fanny suffered so much from being treated as a servant that evening that, despite the exigencies of the situation, she called it the most embarrassing experience of her life. At another time, when a cabriolet broke down, Fanny and her friends were sheltered in a simple dwelling by a compassionate peasant woman who not only fed them and made them comfortable for the evening but also protected them by telling several groups of soldiers from Napoleon's advance guard that they were her relatives. The *Diary* captures much of the tension experienced by the fleeing party.

Several days later, when Fanny was finally safe in Brussels, she was reunited with her husband, who had survived despite a severe illness suffered from riding interminably with little sleep through torrential rains and violent storms. Now assigned a post at the frontier city of Trier (Treves) to recruit, process, and train deserters from Napoleon's army, he came to Brussels to prepare for his mission.

Joyful days followed: sightseeing in the Palais de Lachen, driving in the cabriolet pulled by fine new horses through the Allee Verte, and attending a benefit concert held by the celebrated Madame Catalani. There Fanny observed closely "the king of warriors, Marshal Lord Wellington." She was "charmed with every turn of his countenance, with his noble and singular physiognomy and his eagle eye." Fanny noted that he was gay, animated, gregarious, and enthusiastic. He enjoyed every moment except for the final rendition of "Rule Britannia," the singing of which he considered improper on foreign soil. When his officers "vociferated" for an encore, Fanny soared stylistically to record Wellington's reaction: "He instantly crushed it by a commanding air of disapprobation, and thus offered me an opportunity of seeing how magnificently he could quit his convivial familiarity for imperious dominion when occasion might call for the transformation." [6]

Soon the drives, concerts, and sightseeing ended; d'Arblay left for Trier. Fanny was again separated from her husband but this time she knew that he was relatively safe and she could correspond with him. Left to herself, Fanny roamed the city. Seeing the King and Queen of the Netherlands at church one Sunday, she deplored their "meek and unimportant" demeanor, feeling that it failed "to answer to the representative dignity of their high station, of which they inspire not an idea." On the same occasion, she revealed a rare touch of Burney humor during such solemn days by noting how the Dutch ladies-in-waiting, fearful of attracting attention, "ran skidding down the aisles of the chapel, tip tap, tip tap, like frightened hares, making no sound in their progress. . . ." [7]

Fanny wrote about few individuals during these days in Brussels but compensated by providing several larger scenes from the daily lives of the people. Best of these is her graphic description of a religious parade with a modicum of satire directed against Catholic pomp and pageantry. But Fanny reached her heights in portraying the turbulence, alarm, despair, and final joy of Waterloo. Usually in relating past events she carefully maintained the time sequence. On occasion here in recreating the battle preparations, she commented from her knowledge of results to gain poignancy. For example, she described Brunswick's army marching past her window on its way to the front, adding the observation that neither the general nor most of the men survived. Generally, however, she related incidents as they occurred, effectively creating both suspense and immediacy.

Underlying Fanny's entire account is her antipathy towards the Belgians. They watched curiously but placidly as the English soldiers passed by: "no kind greeting welcomed their arrival; no warm wishes followed them to combat." [8] Standing in the midst of the Belgians, Fanny could not determine whether they were Bourbonists or Bonapartists, such was their passivity. As the sound of cannon grew louder and as more soldiers marched to the front, the dearth of news was frustrating. Fanny viewed the lack of information as additional proof of the people's insensitivity and apathy. Surely there was word from the battlefield! Why was it not announced? Gazettes would have been hawked in London streets; bulletins would have been posted in Paris; but nothing was done in Brussels.

Consequently, confusion fed by rumor grew. One day while Fanny heard an uproar outside, someone burst into her room, shouted that "*the French were come,*" and fled before she could see him. Quickly she crammed her money and papers into a basket, threw on her shawl and bonnet, flew down the stairs, and dashed into the street. Unable to get through the crowd to her friends, the Boyds, she sought refuge with a French acquaintance. Here she passed "a dreadful day," waiting fearfully, knowing nothing, and surmising the worst. Even as she recapitulated the experience years later, Fanny was still haunted by "the horrible apprehension of being in the midst of a city that was taken, sword in hand, by an enemy—an apprehension, that, while it lasted, robbed me of breath, chilled my blood, and gave me a shuddering ague." [9]

Finally, during "the turbulence, the inquietude, the bustle, the noise, the cries, the almost yells," Fanny's fears were relieved by Mr. Saumarez, an English commissary just returned from the battlefield. He provided news of initial successes and what seemed to be an "exaggerated panegyric" of Wellington. The Duke had been everywhere: "the eye could turn in no direction that it did not perceive him either at hand or at a distance; galloping to charge the enemy, or darting across the field to issue orders." Although constantly shot at, he seemed "as impervious for safety as he was dauntless for courage." [10]

Soon Saumarez's favorable report was verified by more complete accounts of the glorious Allied victory. But Fanny was overwhelmed by the tragic aftermath of Waterloo. For more than a week she viewed nothing from her window but "maimed, wounded, bleeding, mutilated, tortured victims. There seemed to be a whole and a large army of disabled or lifeless soldiers." [11]

She was stricken at the sight of wounded prisoners biting their own clothes or flesh to stop groaning. Almost as sad was "the remorse and madness" of their healthy comrades, now wishing that they had been killed instead of being forced to parade through the city that Napoleon had expected to conquer.

To take care of the staggering number of wounded, churches and private homes were used. Fanny's friends were busy "nursing, dressing wounds, making slops, and administering comfort amongst the maimed, whether friend or foe." [12] She herself spent half of every day making lint or working among the wounded. Hardest to endure was the mephitic odor engulfing the entire city. To eliminate it, three thousand peasants were employed to bury the dead on the plains. Even so, everyone—"even amongst the shopkeepers, even amongst the commonest persons"—frequently used eau de Cologne or vinegar.

Eventually Brussels ceased serving as an "out-doors hospital." Life began to take on a more normal routine. Sightseers arrived from all countries to inspect the battlefield and to hear details of Wellington's "immortal victory." An enervated Fanny longed for a return to the peaceful country life of West Humble. Her present "wandering, houseless, emigrant" existence was an anathema to her. She put it succinctly: "This is no siècle for those who love their home, or who have a home to love." Then she buried the thought in an avalanche of rhetoric: " 'Tis a siècle for the adventurous, to whom Ambition always opens resources; or for the New, who guess not at the catastrophes that hang on the rear, while the phantom Expectation allures them to the front." [13] Her own time for peace was not yet at hand.

II *An Injury Leads to Death*

One afternoon almost a month after Waterloo, Fanny received word from Trier that her husband had been severely kicked in the leg by a wild horse, and that the resulting wound had been further aggravated by an inept surgeon. Despite the danger of traveling because the routes were infested with desperate fugitives from Napoleon's army and pillaging Prussian soldiers, she left almost immediately. Harassments and vexations marked her trip, which lasted for five days and covered over two hundred twenty-five miles instead of the usual one hundred twenty. Fanny slept and ate little; she grew depressed with the constant heavy rain and the ubiquitous scenes of "straggling soldiers, poor, lame or infirm labourers, women, and children." Scarcely a healthy man could be seen among the civilian population. Fanny had no illusions about the glory and grandeur of war, having witnessed in Brussels and in this trip across country the misery, suffering, deprivation, and hardship during and following Waterloo. Fortunately, she did not experience great distress herself. With courage, determination, and an indifference to personal safety, she finally reached her husband, who, although not well, was out of danger.

Several weeks later, the d'Arblays returned to Paris. With her penchant for stumbling across famous figures, it is not surprising that Fanny, while stopping briefly at Chalons for half a day, encountered the Russian Emperor, Alexander I. He was walking in front of an old house, without any crowds, guards, or signs of grandeur, wearing an "undress" uniform devoid of stars or decorations. Fanny was impressed with his "hilarity, freedom, youthfulness, and total absence of all thought of state or power," which made him seem like "a jocund young Lubin, or country esquire. . . ." [14] Otherwise the trip was uneventful although General d'Arblay found it humiliating because his personal passport was not recognized at the French border, and he had to search in his *portefeuille* for the Allied one issued with his letter of recall. In addition, the roads near Paris were lined with English sentinels, guards, and soldiers, causing the d'Arblays to ride in silence, astonished "on re-entering the capital of France, to see the vision of Henry V revived, and Paris in the hands of the English!" [15]

From the time of her return to England in the fall of 1815,

Fanny's *Diary* is relatively incomplete, uninteresting, and unimportant. Having lost Camilla Cottage due to legal complications, she and her husband settled in Bath. Here among other old friends she met Mrs. Piozzi but failed to renew their former intimacy despite an exchange of visits and letters. During one of several trips to Bath by the Queen, Fanny presented her husband to Charlotte. The scene is described at length as d'Arblay, dressed in full uniform with his military decorations, met the gracious, courteous, and friendly Queen for the first time. With an arch smile Her Majesty told him, "Madame d'Arblay thinks I have never seen you before! but she is mistaken, for I peeped at you through the window as you passed to the terrace at Windsor." [16]

Except for Fanny's graphic description about being trapped with her dog, Diane, in a cavern surrounded by slowly rising water during a summer storm, the final pages of the *Diary* concern mainly the deaths of loved ones. The hardest loss was naturally that of her husband, who had never fully recovered from illnesses suffered during the Hundred Days and afterwards. He endured his lengthy sickness with the fortitude and nobility that characterized his life. During his final days, he talked to Fanny about her future. Among other matters, he requested her to speak often of him to his son so that Fanny's fame would not completely eclipse his memory. Most poignant was d'Arblay's statement on May 3, 1818: "Je ne sais si ce sera le dernier mot . . . mais ce sera la dernière pensée—*Notre réunion!*" ("I know not if this will be the last word . . . but it will be the last thought—*Our reunion!*"). Appropriately, those were his last words. Under such circumstances one may excuse Fanny's rhetorical sentimentalizing: "Oh, words the most precious that ever the tenderest of husbands left for balm to the lacerated heart of a surviving wife." [17]

Fanny was grief-stricken again in November when the Queen passed away. At the funeral service, she "wept the whole time, as much from gratitude and tenderness to hear her [the Queen] thus appreciated as from grief at her loss. . . ." [18] During the next five years Fanny also lost her brother James, her cousin Charles Rousseau Burney, and her old friend, Mrs. Piozzi. She gained, however, her desire to write again, and set down from memory and memorandum many events that had occurred to her before, during, and following Napoleon's Hundred Days. In addition, she resumed the arduous task of assorting, collating, and arranging the voluminous papers and correspondence that were to comprise her father's memoirs.

III   *Glorification of Father*

Fanny had originally commenced working on Dr. Burney's memoirs as a labor of love; she ended thirty-five years later burdened by a task that frustrated, enervated, and overwhelmed her. During this period the pleasant, cooperative venture of assorting and discussing materials with him, begun about 1797, turned into an exasperating, lonely occupation after the deaths of her father and husband when, in 1820, she devoted herself entirely to editing the voluminous papers. Then she became fully aware of their shortcomings. The material about Dr. Burney's early life dealt mainly with unpleasant memories of his parents; the material about his early manhood concerned unknown and uninteresting people; and the material about his London life consisted primarily of lists of engagements, people met, places dined at, homes visited, and the like.

By 1828 Fanny had gone through all the bags of letters, memoranda, notes, and scraps; had consulted Esther before burning whatever would be embarrassing to her father or family; and had decided upon a three-volume work comprised mainly of letters written by eminent people to him. She had to abandon this plan upon learning that the new copyright laws, passed when she was in France, classified letters as literary works, thereby preventing their being published without permission of the authors. This information, along with the notification that another person was planning to write about Dr. Burney unless Fanny did so, caused her to discard her previous project and begin anew. Three years later she finished. In 1832, when Fanny was eighty, *The Memoirs of Dr. Burney* appeared in three volumes. A fourth, referred to throughout the work as "The Correspondence," was designed to contain letters written to and by her father, but it never materialized because of Fanny's advanced age and her annoyance about the unfavorable reviews.

The Memoirs does not contain much material written by Dr. Burney, as originally planned. Nor does it reprint the many interesting letters written to him by famous people. Instead, it is a typical eighteenth-century Life, idolatrizing the subject and edifying readers, and characterized by sparse information about his youth, by insertions of extraneous material, and by didactic passages. Specifically, Fanny portrayed her father as a symbol of The Successful Self-Made Man. Born to neither Wealth nor Rank, in fact raised as an Abandoned Child, he persevered through Industry and Merit until he achieved well-deserved fame. Just as Fanny's heroines broke through class barriers, so Dr. Burney rose from a menial apprentice to a loved and respected member of cultured London society.

It is this accomplishment, this portrait of her father as a self-made man who had climbed up the ladder of success, that Fanny admired and gave as the *raison d'être* of the work. In her preface she stated that *The Memoirs* would interest readers wishing to trace "the progress of a nearly abandoned child from a small village of Shropshire, to a Man allowed throughout Europe to have risen to the head of his profession; and . . . to have been elevated to an intellectual rank in society, as a Man of Letters. . . ." [19] As Fanny stressed, attaining success demanded arduous, exhausting work. Dr. Burney labored long, hard hours to feed, clothe, house, and educate his large family. Fanny discloses how he utilized to advantage almost every moment of his early and middle years by telling, for example, about his learning Italian while traveling on horseback from one music pupil to another, dictating to his daughters although ill in bed, and writing until the wee hours of the morning after giving music lessons from dawn.

Dr. Burney's *Memoirs* illustrates the ethic that ability and perseverance enable one to rise from the lowest to the highest circles. In this ascent, moral character also plays a vital role. Although Fanny never shows Dr. Burney confronted with any problem, or having to choose between what is expedient and what is right, she does point to his having resisted the seductive appeals of gambling, luxury, and "dangerous pleasures" while an apprentice to Fulke Greville. She emphasizes that "a love of right was the predominant feature of the mind of young Burney," [20] overlooking his inability to afford any of the expensive vices.

Added to Dr. Burney's industry and virtue was his charm. He was known to enter homes as a music teacher and to depart as a friend. Dr. Johnson called him a man "for everybody to love," adding that "it is but natural to love *him!*" [21] What made Burney so lovable or likable is never fully revealed. He appears to have been an unpretentious, unsophisticated man, interested in people and their pursuits, well read, widely traveled, intelligent, tolerant, cheerful, and loyal to his friends. To those suspicious of his motives, like Mrs. Thrale, he may have appeared obsequious. Yet he numbered too many great men of his day among his personal friends to have deceived all of them for so long. Unfortunately, Fanny never portrays him talking for any period of time to others. Often if he is a member of a group, she relates what was said to him rather than what he states. Ironically, Dr. Burney, the subject of *The Memoirs*, is not presented so dramatically or so graphically as Johnson, Burke, Garrick, and others.

The work suffers from other blemishes. If Fanny was aware of her father's faults, she gave no indication of it. She acknowledged that *The Memoirs* was more of a panegyric than a comprehensive analysis of Dr. Burney, but she pleaded that truth was not wanting in her account, just "vice and frailty" in her father. Only once does the tone deviate slightly from adoration. On this singular occasion, Dr. Burney forgot protocol in his absorbing discussion with the King. Fanny wrote that "no one at all accustomed to Court etiquette could have seen him without smiling" and then refers to him as "an unsophisticated character" although in the favorable sense of being natural, unpretentious, and unaffected.[22]

Just as Dr. Burney never seems real because of Fanny's failure to present him dramatically and to portray his faults, so she never sets forth his ideas on life. One wonders what specific words of wisdom or general reflections about life and people he provided that enabled the Burneys to become one of the most admired and respected families of the period because of their accomplishments in literature, music, and scholarship. Fanny is never concerned with this aspect of her father; she never examines his influence as a parent. One must conclude that the children assimilated his qualities by working with him and by watching him work. In this fashion they developed his desire for excellence and his willingness to labor in attaining it. No other lessons were needed.

Yet he did pass on to them his tolerant and sympathetic attitude towards his fellow man. Late in his life he noted that his most flattering letters had come from Dr. Johnson and Rousseau, men of widely divergent views. Although aware of the weaknesses and shortcomings of these great figures, Burney always treated them with "regard and reverence." He could not understand why others acted as if "the characteristic of human nature were perfection, and the least diminution from it were unnatural and unpardonable." [23] Armed with this attitude, Burney made friends easily and kept them.

IV *Picture of an Era*

Although *The Memoirs* is not a significant biographical work, it does provide interesting and valuable material for literary, political, and social historians. Arranged in chronological order as a series of character sketches of people who played a prominent part in Dr. Burney's life, the work depicts numerous famous individuals of the period. Much of the material, however, adds little to what has since been published in the *Early Diary* and the *Diary*. Usually editions of these works contain excerpts from *The Memoirs* in footnotes or addenda. With the exception of scenes depicting Garrick, the accounts written by the younger Fanny in the diaries are superior to similar ones in her last work.

Among the material not to be found elsewhere in Fanny's writings is a charming correspondence between her father and Dr. Johnson before the latter was particularly well-known.[24] From the small town of Lynn Regis, Burney wrote in 1755 to the editor of the *Rambler* and *Idler* to express his praise of Johnson's "periodical productions"; to inquire about "the admirably planned, and long wished-for Dictionary"; and to apologize for taking up his time by pointing out that "it is the fate of men of eminence to be persecuted by insignificant friends as well as enemies." Johnson's reply to the amiable inquiry is a model of courtesy and eloquence. He begins by stating that the delay in answering is not due to any desire to neglect Burney. Instead, he enjoys hearing from a person whose "civilities were offered with too much elegance not to engage attention." Moreover, he states that "few consequences of my endeavors to please or benefit have delighted me more than your friendship thus voluntarily offered."

As to the *Dictionary,* Johnson referred Burney to the publisher, Dodson; but he added that, after reading the work, Burney should write: "If you find faults, I shall endeavor to mend them; if you find none, I shall think you blinded by kind partiality." Seizing upon this flattering and friendly reply as an invitation to correspond regularly, Burney dispatched another letter. Johnson failed to answer this one or another written two years later praising the *Dictionary* but expressing regret at learning of his plan to edit Shakespeare. Burney felt that a man with Johnson's genius should not engage in the "dull drudgery of carrying rubbish from an old building" but should be "tracing the model of a new one."

Unfortunately Burney did not keep any detailed records of his first meeting with Dr. Johnson or of subsequent ones. An intimacy developed between these two men during the Streatham years, especially on their trip together to Winchester School, where Johnson introduced Burney and his son, Richard, a student there, to Dr. Warton. During their visit together en route and during another that the two men took to Oxford so that Johnson could introduce his many friends to Burney, a close friendship was formed.

Although Dr. Burney provides no new information or anecdotes, Fanny does. One story concerns Johnson's lack of practical information about diseases and remedies. According to Fanny, once during the middle of his life, upon finding himself suffering from gout, he plunged his leg into a pail of cold water, "a feat of intrepid ignorance—incongruous as sounds the word ignorance in speaking of Dr. Johnson. . . ." It was undoubtedly the act of a desperate man trying to do something about one of the many illnesses plaguing him during his whole life. Dr. Burney had never known Johnson to be free from pain or infirmity. Despite his poor health, or perhaps because of it, he was considerate and kind towards other sufferers.

Fanny also wrote about visiting Bolt Court with her father, where they met Anna Williams. Johnson's sympathetic regard for this blind poetess, and his attentions and courtesy towards her caused Fanny to state that "he never appeared to more advantage" than he had that day. She also mentioned his kindness in housing and supporting Mrs. Desmoulins, the indigent daughter of his godfather; and Mr. Levet, "a poor ruined apothecary."

The other material about Dr. Johnson either repeats episodes and observations previously discussed in connection with the diaries or adds little that is new or different. This same dictum applies to the many other figures, who together make up a *Who's Who* of the period: Reynolds, Burke, Boswell, the Thrales, Goldsmith, Gibbon, Captain Cooke, Horace Walpole, and Sheridan. One new individual in Fanny's work is William Pitt the younger, whose civility caused Dr. Burney to mention that the prime minister "was as obliging as if I had half a dozen boroughs at my devotion." A short time later, Burney, after observing Pitt, concluded that "no one can be more cheerful, attentive, and polite to the ladies than Mr. Pitt." [25] This impression is contrary to the "surly churl" image that many others had of the prime minister.

Another new figure is the Prince of Wales, the future George IV, who enjoyed talking about music with Dr. Burney and about classical literature with his son Charles. The genial spirits of the Prince caused Dr. Burney to break his vow about not drinking. The "irresistible temptation to hobbing and nobbing with such a partner in a glass of cherry brandy" was too much for anyone to resist. Besides, as Dr. Burney added later, the liquor was no stronger than peppermint water. As a result of such conviviality, Fanny's father was favorably impressed with George's dissolute son. The Prince is described as having "engaging good-humour," being "prompt at polite and gratifying compliments," possessing a fund of "wit and humour," and displaying "more conversational talent, and far more learning than Charles II." Dr. Burney added that there was "no individual, male or female, with whom I talk about music with more sincerity, as well as pleasure, than with this captivating Prince." [26]

V   *Few Family Facts*

Although *The Memoirs* presents a panorama of cultured society in the second half of the eighteenth century, it discloses little about members of the Burney family besides Fanny and her father. A few paragraphs suggest the author's devotion to her mother, Esther Sleepe, who had died when Fanny was ten. The feminist sentiment in the Burney novels, although not radical, may have resulted from Esther's interest in and knowledge about matters not traditionally associated with women. In writing to Johnson about his first wife, Dr. Burney referred to her as a woman "whose intellects are sufficiently masculine to enter into the true spirit of your writings." [27] And again, in verses written after her death, he mentions her as joining "manly sense to female softness."

Reared by such a woman, Fanny was not brought up to be confined to the kitchen or bedroom but was well prepared for the drawing rooms at Streatham, the ceremonies at Windsor, the sparsities at Camilla Cottage, and the vicissitudes at Brussels. In addition, her heroines reflect the image of Esther Sleepe by being women who assert themselves instead of remaining as weak, passive, helpless creatures. Despite the paucity of material about Fanny's mother, which might have been expanded with the help of other family members, what is preserved suggests the vital role that she played in the household, and the influence that she had on Fanny.

Almost completely ignored in *The Memoirs* is Dr. Burney's second wife, Mrs. Stephen Allen. Fanny was not adverse to her father's remarrying; in fact, she specifically states that a person's doing so does not reveal "any want of feeling" but signifies merely that he is "consenting to receive such good as is attainable, while bowing down submissively to such evil as is unavoidable." Despite her reconciliation with and even approval of her father's second marriage, neither she nor the other children, as has been previously discussed, ever liked their stepmother. There is a soupçon of malice in Fanny's relating how Mrs. Allen engaged Dr. Burney to give her daughter music lessons, scheduling them at tea time so that, "when liberated from the daughter, he might be engaged with the mother." [28] However, Fanny did not allow personal enmity to color the account of her father's relationship with his second wife. Dr. Burney loved and was devoted to her; she made an excellent wife even though she left much to be desired as a stepmother.

Other members of the family are ignored. No significant mention is made of Charles, who was famous for his classical library and scholarship; of James, who was promoted to Rear Admiral, was the author of several books about his voyages and one on whist, and was a close friend of Lamb, Wordsworth, Coleridge, and other literary figures; or of Sarah Harriet, Fanny's half-sister, who published three novels and other works. Such omissions, as Scholes points out, are serious; but he is hardly justified in terming them "a rather shocking example of senile vanity." [29]

VI *Ire of the Critics*

Yet *The Memoirs* has always provoked critics into using strong language. It is ironic that Fanny's lifelong desire to remain anonymous, or at least to shun any publicity or controversy, should have been realized during most of her lengthy career but not after her eightieth year. Publication of *The Memoirs* precipated a scathing attack by John Wilson Croker in the *Edinburgh Review*.[30] He particularly castigated its "pompous verbosity" and other stylistic weaknesses. Even more damaging was his charge that the work was deceptive in being Fanny's own biography instead of her father's.

As for the matter of style, Croker is correct. *The Memoirs* is written in a grandly eloquent manner with circumlocutions, pompous phrases, involuted sentences, stilted diction, personification, epic similes, and elaborate constructions. Obviously the style is intended to convey a sense of dignity and grandeur to the subject; unfortunately, it fails dismally. Its artificiality is particularly noticeable because *The Memoirs* includes many old letters written by Fanny and her father in the natural, sprightly, unpretentious, informal manner of *Evelina* and the diaries. Compared with them, the many pages written by the aged Fanny form a sharp contrast and appear even more markedly obfuscating. There is no doubt but that Croker's criticism about style is sound.

Croker's second charge—that the memoirs of Dr. Burney were actually Fanny's—is ungracious and somewhat inaccurate. Fanny's life, especially after she wrote *Evelina*, was so intertwined with her father's that it would have been virtually impossible to have separated them completely. In addition, she clearly stated in her preface that, although her father was to be the central figure in the work, she had also included "characteristic details about celebrated personages," which she felt would interest "the youthful reader." Specifically, she asked to be excused for such "apparent egotisms" as appeared in writings about herself and Dr. Johnson, Burke, and others. Whether Croker read the preface or whether he felt that such qualifications should have been indicated by a different title is not clear. What is certain is that Fanny has prepared readers of the preface for what appears in the work. She might, however, have exercised better judgment about some of the material. Many of the sections concerning General d'Arblay, particularly his reunion with General de Lauriston in a London hotel, could easily have been omitted.

Controversy about *The Memoirs* continues. A recent critic has charged among other things that Fanny has corrupted the work by censoring everything unfavorable to Dr. Burney.[31] This criticism is certainly just; but to term Fanny a failure as a "memorialist" and to call *The Memoirs* "reprehensible" is overstating the matter. As a writer of the second rank, Fanny's views on biography were those of her age. She was shocked at Boswell's *Life of Johnson;* she felt clearly, as has been noted, that a man's faults should be forgotten and his virtues preserved. Even Dr. Johnson at the end of his career in writing *The Lives of the Poets* sets forth the same concept although he had previously held a contrary view.[32]

To expect Fanny to relate personal or unflattering details about a father whom she had admired, if not idolized, throughout her life is asking too much of this eighteenth-century author. That she failed to rise to new heights in *The Memoirs* is natural in view of her advanced years. That she wrote in an abominable style is to be expected after her previous work, *The Wanderer*. That she included too much material about herself, her husband, and her experiences with well-known people is to be deplored. Yet such bitter, ill-tempered language on the part of critics is uncalled for. If the diaries had not been published, these individuals would be more thankful for *The Memoirs* and would denigrate the work less.

VII   *The Last of the D'Arblays*

The final years of Fanny's life were sad ones. Her son Alex, previously a disappointing university student, had proved unpopular as a priest in the Church of England because of his desultory habits, forgetfulness, frequent absences, eccentricities, and lethargy. Shortly after he was appointed minister at Ely Chapel in Holborn through Fanny's influence, he contracted influenza and died on January 19, 1837, at forty-three.

Few members of Fanny's family were left. Esther had died five years earlier, leaving only the invalid Sarah Harriet, Fanny's youngest stepsister; and Charlotte Broome, Fanny's sister. The later passed away in about a year. Fanny lived on despite illness and infirmity, often suffering mental lapses but having many lucid moments. Finally, on January 6, 1840, the day when her devoted sister Susan had passed away forty years earlier, Fanny succumbed. During her eighty-seven years, she had lived as full, varied, and stimulating a life as any eighteenth-century woman. Due to her industry, conscientiousness, and ability, much of herself, her family, her friends, and her world remains alive today in her voluminous writings for the enjoyment and information of readers everywhere.

CHAPTER 11

A Recapitulation

FANNY BURNEY'S contributions to literature are three-fold: (1) writing an important novel, *Evelina*, that continues to be read and admired; (2) influencing the direction of fiction by fusing the tradition of Fielding, Richardson, and Smollett in a new genre—the novel of manners; and (3) preserving in her diaries, journals, and letters much of the spirit and many of the people of the age.

Such accomplishments are not sufficient to rank Fanny among the period's great figures. She contributed neither a major masterpiece, as did Pope, Swift, Boswell, Sterne, Fielding, and Richardson; nor several significant works, as did Johnson, Goldsmith, Smollett, Addison, and Steele. Lacking the critical perception and judgment of these writers, she failed to realize what she did well and what poorly. Unlike them, she manifested little interest in literature, its theory, or its application. While Richardson advanced from *Pamela* to *Clarissa*, Fielding from *Joseph Andrews* to *Tom Jones*, and Smollett from *Roderick Random* to *Humphrey Clinker*, Fanny deteriorated from *Evelina* to *The Wanderer*. Unable to recognize the nature and range of her special but limited talent and without critical guidance from others, Fanny left a corpus of work worthy of only a secondary place among English literary figures of the eighteenth century.

I *Novelist*

Yet that place is rightfully secure. Critical articles continue to be written about *Evelina*, and its publication recently as a paperback suggests that it is still widely read.[1] But Fanny's first novel needs no such external evidence to substantiate its merits. As social comedy it speaks for itself. Although the work is marred by didactic passages, a wooden hero, a melodramatic subplot, and some sentimentality, the refreshingly natural heroine and the

gently satirical representation of various middle-class characters
provide an amusing picture of the manners at that time and in all
times. Conformity is as necessary for social acceptability today as
in the eighteenth century. In a sense, Evelina is Everygirl, striving
not like Everyman for admission to heaven in the hereafter, but
for heaven in the here—namely, entrance into a sorority, womans
group, country club, or social clique. Fanny balances the seriousness of the social problem with satire at the expense of those
pretending to be acceptable but obviously unqualified. The
Smiths and Branghtons are prototypes of the aspiring middle
class, trying to ape the forms but lacking the grace and decorum
of the gentility. Fanny's snobbish views are made more palatable
by her also subjecting the upper classes to the malice of her
satire. Few are spared from her perspicacity. The result is that
Evelina combines the charm of its sensitive young heroine with
the comic vision of an author who was a shrewd and keen ob-
server of people and their foibles.

Fanny's later novels departed from this successful format. The
sprightly first-person narrator was replaced by an obtuse, stilted,
verbose, omniscient author who intruded with increasing fre-
quency to comment on the action and on the characters, or to
proffer social instruction. The simple plot relying on the interaction of characters grew more and more complicated, depended
more and more on chance and coincidence, and consisted more
and more of melodramatic situations. The heroines became less
natural and interesting; the heroes continued to be artificial and
pretentious. With a few exceptions, particularly Sir Hugh Tyrold
in *Camilla*, other characters were types and caricatures. Fanny's
deterioration may be attributed to her turning from satirical to
serious fiction, and from writing about the world that she knew to
a world beyond her. These changes may well have resulted from
her bitter discouragement following the antipathy of her father
and Crisp to her first unpublished play, *The Witlings*. Only in a
later comedy, *A Busy Day*, did she return to the tightly constructed comedy of manners suited for her talent.

Fanny Burney's importance as a novelist depends only in part
upon *Evelina* and other works; in part it rests upon her influence
on the development of the novel. The mention of Richardson,
Fielding, and Smollett in the preface of *Evelina* indicates her own
awareness of an indebtedness to these authors. Clearly, she drew

from them. In Richardson may be found the epistolary style, the feminine perspective, the plot about a young girl's problems, and the sentimental tendencies. The similarities between *Evelina* and Richardson's *Sir Charles Grandison* are numerous: Evelina's letters are like those of Emily Jervois, Lord Orville is in the tradition of Sir Charles, and Mrs. Selwyn has the tongue of Charlotte Grandison. Most interesting is that both young heroines—Evelina and Harriet Byron—leave the seclusion of the country for London, where they are amused by the people and manners of the town, and besieged by suitors. In Fanny's second novel, Cecilia's madness appears to have been based upon that of Clarissa. Yet for all these parallels Fanny is not one of Richardson's "ladies."

Having been exposed to Fielding, Fanny could not settle for Richardson's simple morality, his introspection, his isolated characters, and his narrow world. She shared Fielding's genial view of humanity, finding amusing people everywhere. Like him, she represents life in many places and on varied levels. Unable as a respectable woman to know about the jails, the inns, the taverns, and the gambling houses, she portrayed instead the feminine world of drawing rooms, millinery shops, mercers, tea tables, balls, ridottos, and boudoirs. Like Fielding, she represents life in the city and the country, among high and middle society, with a sprinkling of lower class characters. Both writers conceived of the novel as an opportunity to present a satirical panorama of their eighteenth-century world.

Fanny and Fielding also shared a realistic, non-sentimental philosophy. Richardson's heroines reveled in self-pity; they probed the recesses of their souls, analyzing minutely their delicate feelings. Fanny and Fielding refused to allow their heroines such emotional orgies. Their women are not pure sensitive souls, given to melancholy and attuned to exquisite notes of refinement and sensitivity. They are devoid of subtle shades of feeling and unhindered by inner hesitancies. Like Fielding's Fanny, Sophia, and Amelia, Fanny Burney's Evelina, Cecilia, Camilla, and Julia are all courageous, resolute, and robust women who are far different from the weak, passive, helpless creatures of Richardson. Nearly all the heroines are put to the test by would-be ravishers. Those of Richardson usually faint; the others fight back. Linked to this portrayal of women is Richardson's narrow and moral philosophy based on chastity. In his novels, nothing seems as important in life

as preserving virginity before marriage. Fielding ridicules this
view effectively in *Tom Jones,* showing that sexual immorality,
while not to be condoned, may be far less sinful than other vices.
Fanny's views are not so liberal, but her heroines have little difficulty with rakes, indicating that to her, young girls had many
other things to worry about.

From Fielding as well as from Smollett, Fanny may have derived her comic types and use of farcical incident. Captain Mirvan
in *Evelina* and the Admiral in *The Wanderer* might easily have
appeared in the pages of *Roderick Random* or *Peregrine Pickle.*
The brutal practical jokes on Madame Duval and Lovel are reminiscent of Smollett's rowdy realism, as are several scenes in *The
Wanderer.* But it is the dozens of auxiliary characters peopling the
novels of Fielding, Smollett, and Fanny Burney that indicate all
are writing in a similar vein. While Smollett is more inclined to
the grotesque and the caricature than the other two, all utilize
exaggerated types, "humour" characters, and deviates from the
social norm for comic effect.

Although Fanny synthesized much from Richardson, Fielding,
and Smollett, she also added a significant new element. Her predecessors were concerned mainly with moral, emotional, sexual, and
physical conflicts. Their central characters struggle to be and do
good, to win another in marriage, to gain wealth, and to escape
the malice of others.

Largely ignoring the omnipresent evils lurking everywhere in
previous novels, Fanny focused on social relationships between
individuals. Her characters strive to gain social acceptance. Danger in their fictional world stems not from the rapacious villain,
from the immoral individual, or from emotional weaknesses, but
from social predicaments brought about by unwillingly associating
with vulgar people, by unknowingly violating social conventions,
and by innocently ignoring prudent conduct. The central situation
in Fanny's novels concerns the heroine's efforts to gain the social
approval necessary to marry the hero. Impeding forces are the
heroine's family (known or unknown), her breaches of etiquette,
her faults of inexperience, and her vulnerability to the malice and
snobbery of others. After suffering countless embarrassments and
humiliations, the persevering heroine benefits from fortuitous circumstances to overcome all obstacles and marry the hero.

Great writers frequently are preceded by lesser ones who indicate the route to take but cannot travel it themselves. So Fanny Burney showed Jane Austen the plan for the novel of manners, leaving it to her to explore and map out the new terrain. Jane Austen possessed the irony, the psychological penetration, the subtlety, and the technical artistry that Fanny lacked. Furthermore, even though both had the comic vision to see the ridiculous in the world around them, only Jane Austen maintained the detachment necessary to portray her heroines' foibles. Yet her indebtedness is such that Virginia Woolf declared that she should lay a wreath on Fanny's grave.[2] To indicate that Jane Austen fell heir to a new tradition, the novel of manners, in no way detracts from her prominence; it serves only to suggest the importance of Fanny's less artistic literary achievement.

More difficult to assess is Miss Burney's role in establishing writing as an acceptable profession for respectable women. Macaulay claims that she "vindicated the right of her sex to an equal share in a fair and noble province of letters." [3] Like many other statements by the Victorian essayist and historian, this one is extreme. As Tompkins points out, women such as Sarah Fielding, Mrs. Griffith, Mrs. Brooke, and others were actively writing, although they had to plead poverty or moral zeal as motivation rather than crass ambition.[4] Fanny similarly hid behind edifying purposes and was spurred on in the writing of at least her last two novels by economic factors, but she dignified woman's place in the novel-writing world. As one whose moral conduct had been impeccable enough to warrant a position in the royal household, and whose third novel was dedicated to the Queen, Fanny Burney could be emulated by other women who previously might have considered writing a novel to be suited only for men and adventuresses. Although Fanny's influence in establishing the profession of letters, particularly novels, as a respected vocation or avocation for women cannot be accurately estimated, it undoubtedly was considerable.

II *Diarist*

Less difficult to evaluate are Fanny's diaries. She was fortunate in having an eventful life, one that in its outlines is as improbable as those of most of her heroines. The story of the unknown girl who wrote a famous novel, associated with Dr. Johnson and other cultivated figures, served as a member of the royal household, married a refugee French general, lived in Paris during Napoleon's reign, waited anxiously near Waterloo for the results of the epic battle, and continued writing and publishing throughout most of her eighty-seven years is more typical of fiction than fact. Fanny's diaries, therefore, are enhanced by her unusual and eventful experiences, and by the famous people whom she encountered.

Would her volumes be as interesting reading if her life had been more ordinary and her acquaintances less famous? To ask this question is like wondering what Boswell's journals would be without Johnson, Rousseau, Voltaire, and others. Such idle speculations should be set aside. Her diaries present a varied, interesting, and valuable insight into the period and its personalities. George Sherburn, the eminent eighteenth-century scholar, has referred to them as a "priceless" record of the important figures of the day.[5]

Yet their limitations are many. Fanny was not concerned with philosophical or theological issues, political or social problems, or psychological theories. She was interested in people. Her object was to record their talk, their idiosyncrasies, their foibles, and their mannerisms. She captured them with her keen eye and sharp ear, always aware of the affected, the ridiculous, and the absurd. To portray them effectively, she presented them in dramatic scenes with lengthy conversations that she seemed to recall vividly. Most of her diaries, whether in the form of letters to her family or friends, or journal entries, are written in the lively, vivacious, spontaneous style of a person enjoying life and fascinated by the thrilling and amusing people around her. Her zest proves to be infectious; consequently, her work is seldom dull and nearly always interesting.

Yet certainly one should not claim for it the high literary achievement of similar works; for Pepys' *Diary*, Rousseau's *Confessions*, and Boswell's *Journals* are all superior by virtue of their greater scope, imaginative power, and critical perception. In a genre requiring personal disclosure, Fanny hides to such an extent behind her reserve and prudery that the effect is disconcerting. It is not that diaries should be written only by romantics who will expose their souls, but that the art form calls for directness, freshness, and candor. Fanny's writings leave one often wondering what she truly felt, thought, or believed. The weakness of her diaries results from her failure to maintain the illusion of honesty. By being unwilling or unable to show readers some glimpse of the self behind her various selves, Fanny fails to realize the full potential of the genre.

Much of the same criticism can be directed against her as a letter-writer. Because many sections of the diaries are comprised of letters to Mr. Crisp, her father, and her sisters, Fanny should be considered as one of the practitioners of the art. But her accomplishments are minor, devoid of such distinguishing characteristics as the satirical malice of Lady Montagu, the elegant wit of Horace Walpole, the fastidious taste of Thomas Gray, the polished urbanity of Lord Chesterfield, and the sensitive simplicity of William Cowper. Fanny's letters, particularly the early ones, are refreshing for their vitality and naturalness. Yet as she grew older, her pen became heavier, her reserve increased, and her artistic incentive dwindled due to the death of Mr. Crisp, her only literary critic. If she had maintained her liveliness of style and had continued to write with some of the candor of her youth, the collection of letters might rank among the finest in a period famous for its letter-writers.

Fanny herself is an anomaly in the world that she portrays. In contrast to the colorful characters parading in her pageant of life, she is demure, quiet, sedate, and diffident. This self-effacing representation does much to overshadow her importance and her stature. It fails to suggest the courage and determination that enabled her to endure many tribulations in court life, in her early married life, and in her experiences abroad. It does not reveal the keen mind and the sharp wit of a woman whose close friends and admirers included Johnson, Burke, Sheridan, Reynolds, Garrick, and Mrs. Delany. It tends to obscure her achievement in presenting a highly interesting, amusing, and sweeping picture of life and people in the second half of the eighteenth century. Yet for those who read her diaries, her novels, and her plays, there is no doubt but that Fanny Burney is a minor writer of lasting though limited significance.

Notes and References

Chapter One

1. *The Complete Works of William Hazlitt,* ed. by P. P. Howe (London, 1931), VIII, 209.

2. Frances Burney d'Arblay, *Memoirs of Doctor Burney* (London, 1832), II, 176.

3. *The Early Diary of Frances Burney, 1768–1778,* ed. Annie Raine Ellis (London, 1913), 2 vols.

4. *Ibid.,* II, 144–46.

5. *Ibid.,* 154–55; see also 154, n.3.

6. *Ibid.,* I, 313.

7. *Ibid.,* p. 335.

8. *The Greville Memoirs,* ed. Lytton Strachey and Roger Fulfors (London, 1938), V, 58–59.

9. *Early Diary,* I, 33–39.

10. *Ibid.,* II, 89–99.

11. Chauncey Tinker, *Dr. Johnson and Fanny Burney* (London, 1912), pp. xxi–xxiii.

12. For the Barlow courtship, see *Early Diary,* II, 47–89.

13. For a thorough discussion of this subject, see Hemlow, *The History of Fanny Burney* (Oxford, 1958), pp. 35–40.

14. The diary and letters for 1776 except for some to Mr. Crisp were destroyed; some material is also missing from 1777. Undoubtedly this material concerned Charles' crime. See *Early Diary,* II, 136, 138.

15. *Ibid.,* p. 147.

16. *Ibid.,* p. 41.

17. *Ibid.,* p. 41.

18. *Ibid.,* I, 88.

19. *Ibid.,* p. 13.

20. *Ibid.,* p. 9.

21. *Ibid.,* II, 30.

22. Donald A. Stauffer, *The Art of Biography in Eighteenth Century England* (Princeton, 1941), p. 41.

23. *Early Diary,* I, 265.

24. *Ibid.,* p. 186.

25. *Ibid.*, p. 15.
26. *Ibid.*, II, 143–44.
27. *Ibid.*, p. 101.
28. Hemlow, *op. cit.*, pp. 79–85.

Chapter Two

1. *Evelina,* ed. Frank D. Mackinnon (Oxford, 1930), p. 103.
2. Perhaps not as well known as Richardson's Pamela and Clarissa, and Fielding's Sophia (*Tom Jones*) and Amelia is Mrs. Eliza Haywood's heroine from *The History of Betsy Thoughtless* (1751), who is frequently compared with Evelina. For the most thorough discussion of the relationship between these two novels, see James P. Erickson, "*Evelina* and *Betsy Thoughtless*," *Texas Studies in Literature and Language,* VI (Spring, 1964), 96–103.
3. *Evelina,* p. 150.
4. *Ibid.*, p. 104.
5. *Ibid.*, p. 436.
6. *Ibid.*, p. 29.
7. *Ibid.*, p. 31. Cf. *Early Diary,* I, 163, 265, 186.
8. Will T. Hale, "Madame D'Arblay's Place in the Development of the English Novel," *Indiana University Studies,* III (January, 1916), 6–9.
9. Macaulay, *The Works of Lord Macaulay* (Boston, 1879), V, 312–18, and Ernest A. Baker, *The History of the English Novel* (London, 1934), V, 170, are the more eminent critics singling out Johnson's influence.
10. Fanny may have derived the *ville* from the French *viell* to suggest those upholding old or traditional manners as opposed to the vulgar ways of the *nouveau riche.*
11. *Evelina,* p. 206.
12. See James R. Foster, *History of the Pre-Romantic Novel in England* (New York, 1949), especially pp. 16–18, 220–22.
13. The most thorough discussion of the sentimental heroine may be found in Robert Utter and Gwendolyn Needlam, *Pamela's Daughters* (New York, 1936), chaps. I–VI, VIII–IX.
14. *Diary and Letters of Madame D'Arblay,* ed. Charlotte Barrett and Austin Dobson (London, 1904–5), I, 72.
15. *Evelina,* pp. 223–24.
16. *Ibid.*, p. 174.
17. *Ibid.*, p. 80.

Chapter Three

1. *Evelina* went through four editions in two years. For a detailed discussion, see Mackinnon's introduction in his edition previously cited.

2. The original edition was edited by Madame d'Arblay and her niece, Charlotte Barrett, and published by Henry Colburn in seven volumes in 1843. The edition referred to in this book (see above) appeared in six volumes.

3. *Diary*, I, 34.

4. Macaulay, *op. cit.*, V, 272.

5. *The Monthly Review*, LVIII (April, 1778), 316.

6. *Diary*, I, 38.

7. *Ibid.*, p. 49.

8. *Ibid.*, pp. 51–56.

9. *Thraliana, the Diary of Mrs. Hester Lynch Thrale (Mrs. Piozzi), 1776–1809*, ed. Katharine C. Balderston (Oxford, 1942), I, 487. "Tayo" was a term of endearment brought back from Tahiti by Fanny's brother James. Mrs. Thrale's earlier opinion of Fanny was not as favorable, see pp. 368, 443.

10. *Ibid.*, p. 549.

11. *Diary*, I, 503.

12. *Ibid.*, pp. 82–83.

13. *Ibid.*, p. 133.

14. *Ibid.*, p. 117.

15. *Ibid.*, p. 169.

16. *Ibid.*, p. 76.

17. R. Blunt, *Mrs. Montagu* (London, 1908), II, 274.

18. The most thorough account of the Thrale-Piozzi affair may be found in Joseph Wood Krutch, *Samuel Johnson* (New York, 1944), pp. 522 ff. See also James L. Clifford, *Hester Lynch Piozzi (Mrs. Thrale)* (Oxford, 1941), pp. 210–31.

19. *Diary*, II, 251.

20. *Ibid.*, p. 251, n.1.

21. To appreciate her role, see Fanny's letter to Queeney Thrale in *The Queeney Letters*, ed. Marquis of Lansdowne (New York, 1943), pp. 66–117.

22. *Diary*, II, 269.

23. *Ibid.*, p. 273.

24. *Ibid.*, p. 280.

25. *Ibid.*, p. 282.

26. *Ibid.*, p. 91.

27. *Ibid.*, I, 342.

28. *Ibid.*, p. 352.

29. *Ibid.*, p. 344.

30. *Ibid.*, p. 85.
31. *Ibid.*, p. 72.
32. *Ibid.*, p. 118.
33. *Ibid.*, p. 219.
34. *Ibid.*, p. 293.
35. *Ibid.*, p. 312.

Chapter Four

1. Austin Dobson, *Fanny Burney* (London, 1904), p. 101, n.1. Fanny was paid the going market price for a first novel according to J. M. S. Tompkins, *The Popular Novel in England 1770–1800* (Lincoln, Nebraska, 1961), p. 9.
2. *The Witlings, a comedy by a sister of the Order* appears in a 126-page manuscript in the Berg Collection of the New York Public Library.
3. *Diary*, I, 148.
4. *The Witlings*, Act III, n.p.
5. *Ibid.*, Act IV, n.p.
6. *Diary*, I, 259.
7. *Thraliana*, I, 401.
8. Dr. Burney's finances at this time are discussed by Percy A. Scholes, *The Great Dr. Burney* (New York, 1958), II, 56–57.
9. See Clifford, *op. cit.*, p. 205; *Thraliana*, I, 497.
10. *Diary*, I, 477–78.
11. *Thraliana*, I, 505.

Chapter Five

1. *Diary*, II, 86, 147.
2. *Ibid.*, p. 139.
3. See "Miscellaneous Pieces of Manuscript, 1772–1828," Berg Collection, New York Public Library.
4. David Cecil, *Poets and Story-Tellers* (New York, 1949), p. 91.
5. *Diary*, II, 201.
6. Tompkins, *op. cit.*, 79–80.
7. *Cecilia; or, Memoirs of an Heiress*, ed. Annie Raine Ellis (London, 1882), II, 210–27. Fanny stated that this scene was the one "for which I wrote the whole book" (*Diary*, II, 71).
8. *Cecilia*, II, 448–50.
9. *Ibid.*, p. 473.
10. For the relationship between *Cecilia* and Jane Austen's *Pride and Prejudice*, see Q. D. Leavis, "A Critical Theory of Jane Austen's Writing," *Scrutiny*, X (June, 1941), 61–87.

11. Although he fails to discuss Belfield's search for the good life, Howard Lee German has written perceptively about the similarity between *Cecilia* and *Rasselas* in his unpublished doctoral dissertation, "Fanny Burney and the Late Eighteenth-Century Novel" (Ohio State University, 1958), pp. 179–80.

Chapter Six

1. *Diary*, II, 187–90.
2. Hemlow, *op. cit.*, 187–92.
3. *Diary*, II, 316–37.
4. *Ibid.*, p. 363.
5. *Ibid.*, pp. 380–82.
6. *Ibid.*, pp. 462–76.
7. *Ibid.*, III, 374.
8. *Ibid.*, II, 329–30.
9. *Ibid.*, IV, 242.
10. *Ibid.*, pp. 246–47.
11. *Ibid.*, IV, 289–94.
12. Writing about this period, Lecky states that "it is probable that no English sovereign since the first days of the Restoration had enjoyed such a genuine, unforced popularity. . . ." (William E. H. Lecky, *A History of England* [London, 1892], V, 452).
13. Macaulay, *op. cit.*, V, 124–29.
14. *Diary*, III, 436.
15. *Ibid.*, IV, 348.
16. *Edwy and Elgiva*, ed. Miriam J. Benkovitz (New York, 1957).
17. *Hubert De Vere, A Dramatic Tale in Five Parts* survives in manuscript form in the Berg Collection, New York Public Library.
18. *Ibid.*, Act III, n.p.
19. *Ibid.*, Act V, n.p.
20. *The Siege of Pevensey* manuscript is in the Berg Collection, New York Public Library.
21. Fragments of *Elberta* may also be found in the Berg Collection, New York Public Library.
22. Marjorie Lee Morrison, "Fanny Burney and the Theatre" (unpublished Ph.D. dissertation, University of Texas, 1957), pp. 125–35.
23. *Diary*, IV, 490–91.

Chapter Seven

1. *Diary*, V, 35.
2. *Ibid.*, p. 83.
3. *Ibid.*, p. 171.

4. *Ibid.*, pp. 197–98.

5. The Berg Collection in the New York Public Library includes a fifty-five page manuscript entitled "Concerning her Courtship."

6. *Diary*, V, 203.

7. *Ibid.*, p. 247.

8. *Ibid.*, p. 251.

9. *Thraliana*, II, 916, n.1.

10. Typical of present critical reaction to *Camilla* is George Sherburn's statement that Fanny's career as a novelist "really stopped" with *Cecilia* ("Restoration and Eighteenth Century," *A Literary History of England*, ed. Albert C. Baugh [New York, 1948], p. 1034).

11. *Camilla; or, A Picture of Youth* (London, 1796), IV, 399.

12. *Ibid.*, V, 288.

13. *Ibid.*, II, 381.

14. *Ibid.*, p. 302.

15. For Fanny's indebtedness to the courtesy books see Joyce Hemlow, "Fanny Burney and the Courtesy Book," *PMLA*, LXV (September, 1950), 732–61.

16. *Camilla*, II, 128.

Chapter Eight

1. *British Critic*, VIII (November, 1796), 527–36; *Critical Review*, XVIII (September, 1796), 26–40; and *The Monthly Review*, XXI (October, 1796), 156–63, which Fanny refers to in her *Diary*, V, 301.

2. *Diary*, V, 298.

3. *Love and Fashion*, pp. 203–4. The 236-page manuscript is in the Berg Collection, New York Public Library.

4. *Ibid.*, p. 233.

5. I am indebted to Hemlow for pointing out the resemblance to *As You Like It*.

6. *Love and Fashion*, p. 20.

7. *The Woman Hater*, Act V, p. 40. The manuscript is in the Berg Collection, New York Public Library.

8. *Ibid.*, pp. 7–8.

9. *Ibid.*, p. 43.

10. *A Busy Day*, Act III, n.p. The manuscript is in the Berg Collection, New York Public Library.

11. *Ibid.*, Act V, p. 79.

12. *Ibid.*, p. 14.

13. *Ibid.*, Act III, n.p.

Chapter Nine

1. *Diary*, V, 479.
2. *Ibid.*, p. 474.
3. *Ibid.*, VI, 24.
4. *Ibid.*, p. 42.
5. The account may be found in the *Diary* MSS, Berg Collection, New York Public Library.
6. *Diary*, VI, 83.
7. See particularly the article by John William Croker, *Quarterly Review*, XI (April, 1814), 123–30. Other reviews appeared in *The Monthly Review*, LXXVI (April, 1815), 412–19 and *The British Critic*, I (April, 1814), 374–86. A later article by William Hazlitt appeared in *The Edinburgh Review*, XXIV (February, 1815), 320–28.
8. *The Wanderer; or, Female Difficulties* (London, 1814), I, 1.
9. *Ibid.*, II, 404.
10. *Ibid.*, V, 394–95.

Chapter Ten

1. *Diary*, VI, 98.
2. *Ibid.*
3. *Ibid.*, p. 151.
4. *Ibid.*, pp. 157–58.
5. *Ibid.*, p. 162.
6. *Ibid.*, p. 207.
7. *Ibid.*, p. 210.
8. *Ibid.*, p. 218.
9. *Ibid.*, p. 231.
10. *Ibid.*, p. 233.
11. *Ibid.*, pp. 237–38.
12. *Ibid.*, p. 241.
13. *Ibid.*, p. 267.
14. *Ibid.*, pp. 284–85.
15. *Ibid.*, p. 286.
16. *Ibid.*, p. 358.
17. *Ibid.*, p. 368.
18. *Ibid.*, p. 379.
19. *Memoirs of Dr. Burney* (London, 1832), I, viii–ix.
20. *Ibid.*, p. 54.
21. *Ibid.*, II, 18.
22. *Ibid.*, III, 98, 102.
23. *Ibid.*, III, 373.
24. *Ibid.*, I, 120–26.

25. *Ibid.*, III, 275, 278–80.

26. *Ibid.*, p. 358.

27. *Ibid.*, I, 123.

28. *Ibid.*, p. 190.

29. Scholes, *op. cit.*, II, 280.

30. John Wilson Croker, *The Edinburgh Review*, XXIV (February, 1815), 320–33.

31. Miriam Benkowitz, "Dr. Burney's Memoirs," *Review of English Studies*, X (August, 1959), 257–68.

32. In his *Life of Addison,* Johnson in 1781 wrote that "it is surely better that caprice, obstinacy, frolick, and folly . . . should be silently forgotten, than that . . . a pang should be given to a widow, a daughter, a brother, or a friend" (*Lives of English Poets,* ed. George Birkbeck Hill [Oxford, 1905], II, 116). Earlier, however, Johnson had stated that a biography should mention a man's faults (*Boswell's Life of Johnson,* ed. George Birkbeck Hill [Oxford, 1934], III, 154–55). The later views reflect Johnson's opinion because he had pondered the problem while writing biography himself. Except for his *Life of Savage,* in which he was describing a man whose illegitimacy, misfortunes, and debauchery were widely known, Johnson, like Fanny, withheld embarrassing details.

Chapter Eleven

1. See Kemp Malone's "*Evelina* Revisited," *Papers on English Language and Literature,* I (1965), 3–19; James P. Erickson, *op. cit. Evelina* was published (New York, 1965) in the paperback Norton Library edition.

2. Virginia Woolf, *A Room of One's Own* (New York, 1929), p. 113.

3. Macaulay, *op. cit.*, p. 320.

4. Tompkins, *op. cit.*, p. 116.

5. Sherburn, *op. cit.*, p. 1071.

Selected Bibliography

PRIMARY SOURCES

1. Manuscripts

The Berg Collection of the New York Public Library contains manuscripts of *The Diary of Mme. d'Arblay* and the *Early Diary of Frances Burney*, in addition to portions of these works discarded or suppressed by herself or her editors. Also included in the collection are manuscripts of the four tragedies and the four comedies, the *Memoirs of Dr. Burney*, and various notebooks, letters, themes, and sundry items.

Major repositories of other Fanny Burney items, as well as those of her father, brothers, and sisters, are the Barrett Collection in the British Museum, and the private collection of Mr. James M. Osborn of Yale University.

For a comprehensive account of additional Burney manuscripts, see Joyce Hemlow, *History of Fanny Burney*, pp. 496–502.

2. Works by Fanny Burney

Camilla; or a Picture of Youth. London: T. Payne, 1796. 5 vols.

Cecilia; or Memoirs of an Heiress. Edited by ANNIE RAINE ELLIS. London: C. Bell and Sons, 1882. 2 vols.

Diary and Letters of Mme. d'Arblay. Edited by CHARLOTTE BARRETT, revised by AUSTIN DOBSON. London: Macmillan and Company, 1904–5. 6 vols.

The Early Diary of Frances Burney, 1768–1778, with a Selection from her Correspondence and from the Journals of her Sisters Susan and Charlotte Burney. Edited by ANNIE RAINE ELLIS. London: George Bell & Sons, 1913. 2 vols.

Edwy and Elgiva. Edited by MIRIAM J. BENKOVITZ. New York: Shoe String Press, 1957.

Evelina; or the History of a Young Lady's Entrance into the World. Edited by SIR FRANK D. MACKINNON. Oxford: Clarendon Press, 1930.

Memoirs of Doctor Burney. London: Edward Moxon, 1832. 2 vols.

The Wanderer; or Female Difficulties. London: Longman, Hurst, Rees, Orme, and Brown, 1814. 5 vols.

1. Biographies

DOBSON, AUSTIN. *Fanny Burney.* ("English Men of Letters Series.")
London: Macmillan and Company, 1904. Sound, highly readable
account of Fanny's life and literature by a scholar familiar with
eighteenth-century life but handicapped by Victorian critical
tendencies.

HAHN, EMILY. *A Degree of Prudery.* New York: Doubleday and Company, 1950. Incomplete, often snide treatment by a modern,
emancipated woman unsympathetic towards the plight of a sister
writer.

HEMLOW, JOYCE. *The History of Fanny Burney.* Oxford: Clarendon
Press, 1958. Excellent and indispensable.

HILL, CONSTANCE. *Fanny Burney at the Court of Queen Charlotte.*
London: John Lane, 1912.

————. *The House in St. Martin's Street.* London: John Lane, 1907.

————. *Juniper Hall.* London: John Lane, 1904. The books by Constance Hill are factual accounts of important parts of Fanny's life.
Well illustrated.

OVERMAN, A. A. *An Investigation into the Character of Fanny Burney.*
Amsterdam: H. J. Paris, 1933. Psychological analysis from a careful reading. Sometimes amusing but usually sensible and perceptive.

SCHOLES, PERCY A. *The Great Dr. Burney.* New York: Oxford University Press, 1948. 2 vols. Excellent study of Fanny's father with a
great deal of information about her and the other Burney children.

TOURTELLOT, ARTHUR BERNON. *Be Loved No More.* New York: Houghton Mifflin, 1938. Highly impressionistic biography, pleasantly
readable but often inaccurate and extremely incomplete.

2. Critical Studies

BAKER, ERNEST A. *The History of the English Novel.* London: H. F.
& G. Witherby, 1934, V, 154–74. Valuable for portraying Fanny
as an anti-sentimentalist and for its lucid, well-balanced analyses
of her novels.

BENKOVITZ, MIRIAM. "Dr. Burney's *Memoirs,*" *Review of English Studies,* X (1959), 257–68. A vitriolic denouncement of Fanny for
misrepresenting her father's character. Fails to consider eighteenth-
century biographical theory.

CECIL, DAVID. *Poets and Story-Tellers.* New York: The Macmillan
Company, 1949. Best critical study of the novels and the novelist.

ERICKSON, JAMES P. *"Evelina* and *Betsy Thoughtless," Texas Studies in*

Literature and Language, VI (Spring, 1964), 96–103. Sound, penetrating examination of the similarities between these two novels.

GERMAN, HOWARD LEE. "Fanny Burney and the Late Eighteenth-Century Novel." Unpublished Ph.D. dissertation, Ohio State University, 1957. Contains too much theorizing about the novel, and too little analysis of Fanny's novels in the light of the eighteenth-century tradition.

HALE, WILL TALIAFERRO. "Madame D'Arblay's Place in the Development of the English Novel," *Indiana University Studies,* XXVIII (January, 1916). Sensible, well-written discussion of Fanny's style, dialogue, humor, characters, plot, but little explication of the novels.

HEMLOW, JOYCE. "Fanny Burney and the Courtesy Books," *PMLA,* LXV (1950), 732–61. Shows how Fanny's novels, especially *Camilla,* were patterned after the courtesy books. Highly illuminating.

HINKLEY, LAURA. *Ladies of Literature.* New York: Hastings House, 1946. Overstates Fanny's significance and ability; interesting and occasionally valuable.

MACAULAY, THOMAS. "Madame D'Arblay." *Critical, Historical, and Miscellaneous Essays.* Boston: Houghton, Osgood and Company, 1879. Classical essay in Fanny's defense. Brilliant in places, colorful; but not always carefully reasoned.

MACCARTHY, BRIDGET G. *The Female Pen.* New York: William Salloch, 1948. Attributes much of Fanny's intellectual and artistic growth to Dr. Burney's musical evenings attended by heterogeneous and cosmopolitan people. Undervalues influence of Crisp.

MONTAGUE, EDWINE and LOUIS L. MARTZ. "Fanny Burney's *Evelina.*" *The Age of Johnson: Essays Presented to Chauncey Brewster Tinker.* New Haven: Yale University Press, 1949. Discursive, clever dialogue with too much art and not enough matter.

MORLEY, EDITH J. *Fanny Burney.* The English Association. Pamphlet No. 60, 1925. Good, general study.

MORRISON, MARJORIE LEE. "Fanny Burney and the Theatre." Unpublished Ph.D. dissertation, University of Texas, 1957. Although padded in many places (the dissertation disease), this study is fresh, sound, and perceptive.

STEEVES, HARRISON R. *Before Jane Austen.* New York: Holt, Rinehart, and Winston, 1965. Best introduction to the novels because of the graceful style, complete plot summaries, numerous quoted passages, and general sound judgment.

TINKER, CHAUNCEY BREWSTER. Introduction to *Dr. Johnson and Fanny*

Burney. London: Andrew Melrose, 1912. Charming, wise discussion of Fanny's ability with the diarist getting the nod over the novelist.

TOMPKINS, J. M. S. *The Popular Novel in England, 1770–1800.* Lincoln, Nebraska: University of Nebraska Press, 1961. Indispensable for its description of the minor novels during the time when Fanny was writing *Evelina, Cecilia,* and *Camilla.*

WHITE, EUGENE. *Fanny Burney, Novelist.* Hamden, Connecticut: The Shoe String Press, 1960. Occasionally informative; generally mechanical and pedestrian.

Index

Anstey, Christopher, *New Bath Guide*, 45
Armstrong, Dr. John, 23
Austen, Jane, 151

Boswell, James, *Life of Johnson*, 51, 56; Fanny's reaction to, 146; *Journals*, 152
Bruce, James, 24
Burke, Edmund, 54–55, 90–91, 142; reaction to *Cecilia*, 63, 68; relationship with Fanny, 74; Fanny's opinion of, 81–82; *Reflections on the French Revolution*, 90
Burney, Dr. Charles, 14; historian of music, 26; literary influence on Fanny, 26–27; opinion of *Evelina*, 45–46; reaction to *The Witlings*, 00; attitude towards Fanny's marriage, 93–94; Dr. Johnson's opinion of, 139
Burney, Fanny, ancestry and childhood, 15–16; family relationships, 21; predilections in reading, 23; marriage to D'Arblay, 93; life with D'Arblay as reflected in the *Diary*, 117–119; her illness, 120; final evaluation of, 147–153
WRITINGS OF:
Brief Reflections relative to the Emigrant French Clergy, 94
A Busy Day, 112–116, 148
Camilla, 148; subscription list for, 95; public reaction, 95–96; its relationship to *Cecilia*, 96–97; its plot, 96–98; function of its subplot, 99–101; its shortcomings, 101–102; characters, 102–103; general flaws, 104; its critical reception, 105
Cecilia, 62, 84; reaction to it, 63, 74; its relationship to *Evelina*, 64; its focus on financial and marital problems, 64–66; characterization, 66–69; cracks in the craftsmanship, 69–71; sense and sentimentality, 71–72; final analysis of its flaws and virtues, 73
The Early Diary, publication of, 16; characteristics of, 16, 17; the Barlow affair, 17–21; omissions in, 21, 24; relationship to *Evelina*, 26–27, 34
Diary and Letters, 45; portrayal of Fanny in, 46–47; characterization of Dr. Johnson, 50–51; relation to Boswell's *Life of Johnson*, 51; omission of Thrale-Piozzi romance, 52–54; problems of the diarist, 55–57; first meeting with George III and Charlotte, 75; account of life at court, 76–84; opinion of The Queen, 77–78; George III's temporary insanity, 78–79; loyalty to King, 79–80; The Hastings trial, 80–82; final days at court, 88–89; portrait of Napoleon, 118–119; style of the later entries, 130–132; flight from Paris to Waterloo, 131–135; death of husband, 137
Edwy and Elgiva, 84–85; 87, 108; production of, 94; reaction to its performance, 94–95

Elberta, 87
Evelina, 26, 61, 62; conditions of
    its publication, 27; compared to
    The Early Diary, 27; relation-
    ship to The History of Caroline
    Evelyn, 29; unified plot, 29–32;
    use of letters, 32–35; characters,
    35–39; comedy of manners, 39–
    43; its appeal to the middle
    class, 43–44; its reception, 45,
    47–48; Fanny's reaction to its
    reception, 46–47; its relation-
    ship to Samuel Richardson's Sir
    Charles Grandison, 149; its re-
    lationship to Henry Fielding's
    Tom Jones, 150; its relationship
    to Tobias Smollett's novels, 150
The History of Caroline Evelyn,
    14, 26; its relationship to Eve-
    lina, 29
Hubert de Vere, a Pastoral Trag-
    edy, 85–86
Love and Fashion, 105–108; 116;
    its similarities to As You Like
    It, 106; its withdrawal from the
    boards, 108
Memoirs of Dr. Burney, Fanny's
    part in, 138–140; its value for
    literary, political, and social his-
    torians, 141–142; absence of
    family facts, 143–144; critical
    reception, 144–146
The Siege of Pevensey, 86–87
The Wanderer, 150; melodramatic
    plot, 121–123; faulty technique,
    123–124; didacticism, 124–125;
    echoes of the picaresque, 126–
    127; a final analysis, 128–130
The Witlings, 58, 63, 148; its
    satirical bent, 59–60; Fanny's
    reaction to its reception, 61
The Woman Hater, 109–112

Crisp, "Daddy," literary advice to
    Fanny, 22, 26, 27; opinion of The
    Witlings, 60; reaction to Cecilia,
    63
Crutchley, Jeremiah, 62–63

D'Arblay, M., 91–93
de Staël, Madame, Fanny's defense
    of, 91–92
Defoe, Daniel, Moll Flanders, 72
Delany, Mrs., relationship with
    Fanny, 74–75
Digby, Colonel Stephen ("Mr.
    Fairly"), 83–84
Dryden, John, translation of Plu-
    tarch's Lives, 23

Fielding, Henry, Tom Jones, 150

Garrick, David, Fanny's admiration
    for his theatrical ability, 24
George III, 13; temporary insanity
    of, 78–79
Goldsmith, Oliver, Vicar of Wake-
    field, 23

Hastings, Warren, 80
Hawkesworth, Dr. John, 23
Hazlitt, William, 14
Hume, David, History of England,
    23

Iliad, 23

Johnson, Dr. Samuel, 13, 14, 16,
    142; Rasselas, 23, 73; his reaction
    to Evelina, 39, 48; Fanny's por-
    trayal of, 50–52; death of, 54;
    desires Fanny to write a play, 58

Macaulay, Thomas Babington, 151
Marivaux, Vie de Marianne, 23
Middleton, History of Cicero, 23
Molière, 109, 111
Montagu, Mrs. Elizabeth, 55

Odyssey, 23

Pepys, Samuel, Diary, 152
Pitt, William, 142–143

Reynolds, Joshua, 48, 55, 142

Richardson, Samuel, 20; *Sir Charles Grandison*, 149

Rowe, Mrs., *Letters from the Dead to the Living*, 23

Schwellenberg, Mrs., First Keeper of the Robes, 88, 90

Shebbeare, Dr., 23

Sleepe, Esther, 14; influence on Fanny, 143–144

Sherburn, George, 152

Smollett, Tobias, *Humphry Clinker*, 34; *Roderick Random*, 126, 150; *Peregrine Pickle*, 150

Stanyan, *Grecian History*, 23

Sterne, Lawrence, *Sentimental Journey*, 23

Thrale, Mrs.; reaction to *Evelina*, 47–48; interest in Fanny, 48–50; romance with Piozzi, 52–54; desire for Fanny to become a playwright, 58; reaction to *Cecilia*, 63

Twining, Reverend Thomas, 23

Voltaire, *Hemiade*, 23

Wellington, Arthur, first duke of, 133–134

Woolf, Virginia, 151